Contents

Careful! SOMEONE'S LISTENING

SOMEONE'S LISTENING

RECOGNIZING THE IMPORTANCE OF YOUR WORDS

Chuck & Winnie Christensen

MOODY PRESS
CHICAGO

All Scripture quotations, unless noted otherwise, are from the *Holy Bible:
New International Version*. Copyright © 1973, 1977, 1984, International Bible Society. Used by permission of Zondervan Bible Publishers.

Illustrations are by Rick Knox.

Library of Congress Cataloging in Publication Data

Christensen, Chuck.
    Careful!someone's listening :   recognizing the impact of your
words /   by Chuck and Winnie Christensen.
        p.   cm.
    ISBN 0-8024-1621-7
    1. Conversation—Religious aspects—Christianity.
I. Christensen, Winnie.   II. Title.
BV4509.5.C475   1990
241'.672—dc20

1 2 3 4 5 6 Printing/BC/Year 94 93 92 91

Printed in the United States of America

Introduction

One of the summer joys for people who live in urban areas is the Farmers' Market. Each week farmers from outlying vicinities bring their fresh produce to sell. At one market Winnie was perusing the sale table, which was laden with slightly damaged or day-old items. She was looking for green peppers that day, and there were several packages of six peppers for forty-nine cents each on the table. As she was looking them over, the manager of the market came up and said, "Wouldn't you love to get peppers at that price in the winter?"

"I certainly would," Winnie replied. "But look at this package. There's a big hole in that center pepper. It's not visible from the top because the side with the hole has been carefully turned toward the bottom of the tray. The plastic wrap on the package keeps all the peppers in place so you can't see the defect. I found it because I bent the package enough to discover it. For my forty-nine cents I do want six whole peppers."

The manager chuckled and walked away.

We have often gone back to that incident after personal disappointments in our careless use of words and similar disappointments with other Christians. "Whole" Christians exhibit beauty in their character and in their words. It is disillusioning when that beautiful wholeness is marred by the "holes" of harsh, unthinking speech.

God places a high value on words. He revealed His character to us through His Word. Similarly, our words express the reality of who we are inside.

Moses carefully listened to God's words and rehearsed for the people of Israel all of God's commands. He summarized clearly: "Take to heart all the words I have solemnly declared to you this day, so that you may command your children to obey carefully all the words of this law. They are *not just idle words for you—they are your life*" (Deuteronomy 32:46-47; italics added). God doesn't waste His words.

God's words give life. Christians are the people who have accepted those words of life. Negative descriptions of speech —malice, gossip, slander, deceit, lying, hypocrisy, complaining, rivalry, jealousy, envy, pride, unwholesome words, idle words, nonsense, foolishness—are the antithesis of God's character.

We would like to improve the direction and value of our speech. Join us as we ponder dark words that Christians use and explore the process necessary to change those words. We enter that process by opening our inner beings to God's cultivating work. Then our words will match the work of His transforming grace. "For out of the overflow of the heart the mouth speaks" (Matthew 12:34).

1

Words Endure

You must give account on Judgment Day for every idle word you speak. (Matthew 12:36; TLB*)

Have you ever wanted to retract your words? Prominent people sometimes find what they have said behind closed doors or "off the record" published in bold headlines in the next morning's newspapers. Laypeople have heard their careless comments circulated through their workplace or local church with additions or glaring distortions.

About thirty years ago, we attended a Moody Institute of Science demonstration at Moody Church in Chicago. The church was filled to capacity with about four thousand people waiting to hear the program conducted by George Speake. Dr. Speake opened his program with an announcement. To some point in that vast auditorium he had directed a microphone. It had picked up and recorded the conversations in a section of the audience that he did not identify. He then held up a large magnetic tape on which the conversations had been recorded. A hush swept over the four thousand as each person tried to remember what he had said while waiting for the program to

The Living Bible.

begin. Dr. Speake offered to play the tape. No one moved. No one rustled paper. The silence was oppressive. Undoubtedly, many were praying fervently that he would not play that tape.

He didn't. "Instead," he said, "I am going to place this tape on a magnet which will automatically erase every word recorded on it. I'm doing it because I don't think Moody Bible Institute could handle the lawsuits that would follow if I played it." It was an act of mercy, not only for MBI but for all the people whose voices were recorded. An audible sigh of relief rippled through the audience as the magnet did its work.

That demonstration made a lifelong impact on us, not only because of the science demonstration but because of Dr. Speake's emphasis on the impact of words. He had used science to illustrate spiritual truths. His practical illustration depicted how a permanent record of our words is made in the universe.

In a recent conversation with Lyle Phillips, formerly of Moody Institute of Science, we verified our recollections of that event. Mr. Phillips said, "We can scientifically state that there is a visual record of everything we have done, traveling at the speed of light into the universe. Radio astronomy," he added, "deters light objects which we cannot see with normal vision."

Imagine yourself on a planet that is ten light-years away from earth. Visualize where you were, and listen to everything you said ten years ago. Who were you speaking to? What were your facial expressions? How did your voice sound? How many of our past actions or conversations would we honestly like to see or hear again? Even if you do not remember a precise event or conversation, it is on record in the universe. Sound waves create vibration of molecules. Mr. Phillips said that scientists are producing radio telescopes so sensitive that they can constantly receive more and more details about the universe. If human beings can do that, how much more exacting God's recordings must be. God keeps records. He has written books, such as the Book of Life, which contains the name of every individual who has trusted Him (Revelation 21:27).

The prophet Malachi said that God was keeping running notes on what people said as they honored Him. "Those who feared the Lord talked with each other, and the Lord listened and heard. A scroll of remembrance was written in his presence concerning those who feared the Lord and honored his name" (Malachi 3:16). The Lord listened to the conversations of believers and recorded their expressions of love and appreciation for Him. God values positive expressions. How thick would your book of words be if it contained only the positive expressions of your praise and worship?

God also records negative words. Jesus said, "I tell you that men [women] will have to give account on the day of judgment for every careless word they have spoken. For by your words you will be acquitted, and by your words you will be condemned" (Matthew 12:36-37).

There is another striking record of words mentioned in the Old Testament. God warned the Chaldeans, who were plotting against Israel, with these words: "You have plotted the ruin of many peoples, shaming your own house and forfeiting your life. The stones of the wall will cry out, and the beams of the woodwork will echo it" (Habakkuk 2:10-11). God warned the Chaldeans that the very walls and beams of their homes would testify against them.

Years later, Jesus added further impact to that statement when He said, "There is nothing concealed that will not be disclosed, or hidden that will not be made known. What you have said in the dark will be heard in the daylight, and what you have whispered in the ear in the inner rooms will be proclaimed from the roofs" (Luke 12:2-3).

We are familiar with the concept of "bugs," or tiny microphones placed in strategic inner sanctums of sensitive government offices that pick up discussions that are not supposed to be heard beyond those walls. But Mr. Phillips told us that a certain type of coil in an extremely sensitive microphone can even pick up the sound of movement within solid objects. Everything in the universe is in constant motion. Molecules in motion in a table sound different than the molecules in a stone or piece of iron. But regardless of where they are, molecules are always moving. We haven't developed the technology yet to decipher the molecular impact of our voices on solid objects, but we know that is not beyond God's capabilities.

Years ago Dr. Speake referred to the possibility of such sensitive microphones being developed. At that time Winnie thought about the reference in Habakkuk 2 to words being imprinted on the beams of homes. She made that comment to her father, who immediately responded, "Now I understand God's statement to Cain in Genesis chapter four, verse ten, when the Lord said, 'What have you done? Listen! Your brother's blood cries out to me from the ground.'"

In summary, everything we have said and done is on permanent record in the universe and is traveling into the vast expanse. Nothing is lost to God, for He sees, hears, and records everything.

"*I KNOW IT DOESN'T MAKE ANY SENSE, BUT I DISTINCTLY HEARD SOMEONE FROM EARTH SAYING: 'YOU'LL NEVER AMOUNT TO ANYTHING!'*"

In the story of the rich man and Lazarus recorded in Luke 16:19-31 Abraham told the rich man to "remember" events from his lifetime. Abraham knew what those events were. They were on record. But more important, the rich man was going to have to endure the total recall of his life without any hope of changing what he had said or done. Only in this life is forgiveness and cleansing possible. That knowledge should sober us, without frightening us into total silence. The following pages are a challenge to each of us to evaluate carefully the stream of words that flows so freely out of our mouths everyday.

THINK IT THROUGH

Think about the walls that surround you today—in your home, in your job, at school, in your car. Which of your words impressed into those walls would you like to hear again?

Consider the meaning of Psalm 19:12-14, Psalm 90:8, and 1 Corinthians 4:5. Only Jesus Christ provides the magnet that can erase the guilt of the recorded words of the past. Consider 1 John 1:9.

SOMETHING TO DO

Pray: "Lord, too many words displeasing to You have escaped my lips. I pray for Your forgiveness." What else could you pray for in the future?

2
Words Have Power

The tongue has the power of life and death.
(Proverbs 18:21)

Words have power. James warned that an uncontrolled tongue is like a spark that "corrupts the whole person [and] sets the whole course of his life on fire" (3:6).

Words can affect a life forever, either positively or negatively. One woman in her eighties told Winnie, "My mother told me when I was a little girl that I would always be a failure, and that is what I have been all my life—a failure." Those words made a lifelong impact which that woman had been unable to shake even in her old age.

We conducted an informal survey in a group of about a hundred professional men and women ranging in age from twenty-one to forty-one. We asked them about the impact words had made in various stages of their lives. We discovered that in the preschool years mothers had made a greater verbal impact than fathers in a ratio of two to one. Praise, encouragement, love, abuse, and anger from those early years were all vividly recalled.

In grade school mothers' words still had the greatest impact, but teachers began to make inroads in their influence.

Following are some comments from those years that remained clear in these professionals' minds:

"You'd make a good judge."

"You can do it."

"You are a ringleader who is always causing problems."

"Never give up."

"Why can't you get straight A's?"

"You are an exceptionally talented child."

"You aren't that stupid, are you?"

"You're a tough kid."

"Why can't you be like your sister?"

One individual relived the embarrassment of her second grade teacher threatening her in front of the class that she'd tape her mouth shut if she didn't stop talking.

An attorney recalled that his parents had written an inscription in his Bible when he was a child praising him for how much he loved the Word of God. He thought they had overestimated his enthusiasm, but it did cause him to determine to love the Scriptures more.

What words have been fixed indelibly on your mind from those early years before you were twelve? How have they affected you? Winnie recalls that when she was eight, well-meaning relatives, fearing she would be overcome by pride as she primped in front of a mirror, warned, "God will make you ugly if you keep doing that." The comment strongly colored her thinking about herself and also distorted her view of God. Mercifully, as time passed the Lord counteracted that negative input.

Some of the individuals we interviewed were still struggling to overcome harsh comments made in their youth. Others had worked hard to disprove negative statements. Those who had received positive reinforcement early in life had obviously blossomed from the encouragement.

When our children were young, we read a statement by a psychologist that 90 to 95 percent of what we say to children should be positive affirmation, and only 10 to 15 percent should be negative. Unfortunately, we usually reverse those ratios. As parents, we were probably as guilty as our forebears

"IF YOU KEEP PRIMPING IN FRONT OF THE MIRROR LIKE THAT, GOD WILL MAKE YOU UGLY!"

in not being as aware as we should have been about the impact of our thoughtless or harsh statements on a child's life.

One of our friends told us of this incident, which happened in a fast-food restaurant. "I heard a loud, strident voice behind me and turned to see an angry mother yanking her little boy. She was saying in a harsh tone of voice, 'If you don't do as I say, you will drown like your cousin did! He didn't put on a belt with his jeans, and he fell in the water and drowned! Don't you ever forget to put a belt on!' The boy cowered under the barrage of angry words. It was the most awful verbal abuse." If a mother treats a child like that in public there is no telling what level of abuse he may be subjected to at home. "The tongue has the power of life and death" (Proverbs 18:21). Angry words can leave lifelong scars.

We especially appreciate James' words about speech and the tongue because he grew up in the same home as Jesus.

(James is named as one of Jesus' brothers in Mark 6:3.) If ever anyone could have been justified in saying, "Why can't you be more like your brother?" it would have been Mary, their mother. We don't know that Mary ever made such a statement to any of her children, but it must have been hard for her after bearing Jesus, who never talked back or lied or disobeyed, to have other children who were less than perfect.

John 7:5 tells us what Jesus' brothers thought about Him. His younger siblings probably directed many rude and snide remarks at Him. James was probably able to speak so passionately and forthrightly about the damaging effects of an undisciplined tongue because he knew about it from personal experience.

James spoke with equal force about the power that the tongue can have to produce good. He describes that life-giving force in terms of a rudder that keeps a huge ship on course, even in a storm.

Winnie's parents were caught in a typhoon on the Pacific during one of their journeys home from the mission field in China. Their ship lost its rudder and bobbed about at the mercy of the waves, totally powerless to stay on course. Another ship had to come alongside of them to rescue the passengers and crew. Though small in comparison to the rest of the ship, a working rudder is absolutely essential to its progress in either storm or calm.

Horseback riders can identify with James's analogy of the tongue's being like a bit in a horse's mouth. As a freshman in college, Winnie signed up for a beginning class in horseback riding, but she was placed in an intermediate class by mistake. The instructor assured her that she was being given the gentlest mare in the stable, but that mare could tell she had an inexperienced rider on her back and took off at top speed as soon as they left the stable. Winnie hung on for dear life, ignorant about bits and reins. It took several experienced riders to bring that horse under control.

Bits and rudders are essential pieces of equipment. "Likewise," James continues, "the tongue is a small part of the body, but it makes great boasts" (James 3:5). That is not

"ARE YOU TRYING TO TELL ME THAT THIS HUGE SAILBOAT IS STEERED BY THAT INSIGNIFICANT LITTLE RUDDER?"

an idle claim. Though small, the tongue can powerfully influence lives. A persuasive speech can stimulate an audience to action. Chuck recalls ringing words of Winston Churchill and Franklin Roosevelt in World War II that motivated their fighting men to persevere against all odds. Churchill called civilians to view their sacrifices as a high calling in the cause of freedom.

Jesus would certainly have used His verbal power for good in His own home. His words were choice and meaningful. Although it wasn't until after Jesus' death and resurrection that James apparently came to life as a believer, Jesus' words were not wasted on James. They became, instead, the rudder that directed the course of his life.

The next chapter surveys the lives of several Bible characters and their use of words. In the midst of awkward, sometimes dangerous circumstances men and women found mutually supporting words that strengthened them in the crises of their lives.

THINK IT THROUGH

Were you the victim of someone's verbal barbs when you were a child? Will you forgive that person(s) and ask the Lord to heal that memory?

Consider Jeremiah 1:4-8. In what ways would these words give encouragement to Jeremiah?

Think about what you have said today. Have those words been life-giving or destructive? Consider Psalm 64:3; Proverbs 22:11; Colossians 4:6; Titus 2:7-8.

SOMETHING TO DO

Thank the Lord for giving you the insight to encourage someone today.

Write a brief letter to someone who encouraged you when you were young—a parent, sibling, relative, teacher, or friend.

3

Encouraging Words of Friendship

The lips of the righteous nourish many. . . . He who refresh-
es others will himself be refreshed. (Proverbs 10:21; 11:25)

Refreshing, nourishing, supportive—so are words spoken by one friend to another. Encouragement touches chords
deep within us and shows us that friends care and understand.

A retired secretary told us that a simple statement from a
friend both comforted and challenged her to keep active in the
things of the Lord: "I'm glad to see you going on so well since
your husband died so suddenly. You are an encouragement to
me."

An engineer said a friend helped him gain self-confi-
dence when he said, "You are a nice, stable person."

A salesman said he was encouraged when a friend told
him that he was compassionate. He said, "It helped nullify
abusive words from my dad when I was a child."

A registered nurse said that a friend reminded her, "Life
is a constant series of changes, and it's not always fair." Those
words helped her to be more realistic in her expectations and
to put more of her energy into building her personal relationship with Christ.

An announcer at an NBC workshop in Chicago commented on Chuck's work, saying, "Don't take yourself so seriously." On the surface it seemed like criticism, but in reality it encouraged relaxation and confidence through the learning process.

In another setting while Chuck anxiously waited to give his testimony, several gathered for prayer before an evening service. The pastor prayed, "Give your servant the assurance he needs to speak well." Being called a servant of the Lord was an encouragement.

The above statements made by friends are not profound or dramatic. What made them memorable to each recipient was that they were spoken to a specific need.

"A friend loves at all times" (Proverbs 17:17). Loving regard for a friend remains constant no matter how much the circumstances may change. One of the world's classic friendships was that between David and Jonathan. Jonathan was the son of King Saul, and David was a young sheep herder. What brought these young men together was mutual confidence in the living God of Israel.

First Samuel 14 records the story of how Jonathan and his armor-bearer won a battle over the Philistines against enormous odds. It was two against an army encampment, but Jonathan had courageous faith.

David, in similar fashion, faced an enemy all alone against tremendous odds. His confrontation with Goliath and the Philistines is much better known than Jonathan's encounter. David trusted God, however, with the same degree of confidence that Jonathan had exhibited. After David's victory, "Jonathan became one in spirit with David, and he loved him as himself" (1 Samuel 18:1). That was the beginning of a lasting friendship.

When David realized that King Saul intended to kill him, Jonathan listened, even though he couldn't believe what he was hearing (cf. 1 Samuel 20). Jonathan's response was, "Whatever you want me to do, I'll do for you" (v. 4). Jonathan risked his life for his friend. As David fled Saul's constant pursuit, Jonathan found him "and helped him find

"WHAT DO YOU SAY WE GO OVER AND SEE HOW WELL THOSE GUYS FIGHT? I HAVE A FEELING THAT, WITH GOD'S HELP, WE CAN DO SOME SERIOUS DAMAGE."

strength in God." He said to David, "Don't be afraid. . . . My father Saul will not lay a hand on you. You will be king over Israel, and I will be second to you. Even my father Saul knows this" (1 Samuel 23:17). Jonathan was not only content to be in second place, but he had the strength of character to verbally encourage the man who would supplant him.

Those two young men had individually chosen to trust God. Their mutual confidence in the Lord had laid the foundation for their friendship. They were each victims of Saul's jealousy and hostility. David was more a target than Jonathan, but Jonathan had a keen understanding of what his friend was going through and sided with David against his father. They pledged loyalty to each other. Jonathan's loyalty for David never changed, even when it became obvious that he would not succeed his father as king. Those are the factors that molded their friendship.

True friends help one another become the best they can possibly be in the place where God puts them, even if one friend becomes more prominent and well-known than the other. There is no rivalry or hostility in such a relationship. Jonathan didn't feel threatened by David's rising position and popularity because he was secure in who he was. That was especially remarkable in light of his father's insecurities.

Insecurity and self-interest will always hinder us from being encouragers. We spoke with a young man who was about to take a position as an assistant pastor. He was excited about the opportunity; however, he modified his excitement with this comment, "I have to be careful in what I try to do. The senior pastor is afraid that I'm going to take his job away from him." Instead of the older man's encouraging the younger to develop and use his spiritual gifts, the younger man had to walk carefully so as not to appear to be a threat. Such an attitude hinders the freedom the Holy Spirit should have to work in a congregation.

In his book *Toward a Growing Marriage* Gary Chapman lists low self-esteem as one of the primary hindrances to good communication. If you cannot accept the person God has created you to be, your ability to support other people will be affected. Someone has defined self-esteem as the opposite of boastful pride; in contrast, it is quiet confidence, self-assurance, and the ability to accept who you are with thanksgiving to God. If you do not develop that kind of attitude, you will not be able to accept other people as the individuals God has created them to be. That, in turn, will keep you from encouraging them.

Barnabas is a positive New Testament example of reassurance. His name means "son of encouragement," and he was generous and giving. One of the first people he took under his wing was new convert Saul of Tarsus. He vouched for Saul's credibility when other church leaders were still afraid of him (cf. Acts 9:26-29). Later, Barnabas was sent to encourage and strengthen new believers in a town called Antioch. The church grew, and Barnabas sought Saul out to invite him to come and join the work (cf. Acts 11:22-26, 30). It wasn't long before Barnabas and Saul were known as Saul (later Paul) and Barnabas (13:42). Paul quickly took precedence. Barnabas had encouraged Paul to active involvement and leadership in service for Christ. He promoted Paul and didn't stifle him. We are refreshed today by Barnabas's unselfish ministry.

The New Testament begins with the unusual events surrounding the lives of Elizabeth and Mary. As an older woman Elizabeth accepted the role the Lord entrusted to her to bear and rear John the Baptist. Her much younger relative Mary received an even greater honor in bearing Jesus Christ, the promised Messiah. Despite their great difference in age, those two women were good friends. There could easily have been rivalry and jealousy between them, but there wasn't.

When Mary arrived at Elizabeth's home, Elizabeth's husband, Zechariah, was unable to speak, having been struck dumb by an angel when he did not believe God's message to him. About the same time Mary's fiancé, Joseph, was contemplating divorcing Mary because he did not know the full story behind her pregnancy. It had been a stressful time for both women, but it was a time of wonderment and exhilaration as well. Elizabeth greeted Mary with these words: "Blessed are you among women, and blessed is the child you bear! But why am I so favored, that the mother of my Lord should come to me? . . . Blessed is she who has believed that what the Lord has said to her will be accomplished!" (Luke 1:42-45). There is no hint of envy or resentment in Elizabeth's words. She was genuinely thrilled for the honor given to Mary. She was humble and sincere. Her words revealed her attitude of heart.

Mary stayed with Elizabeth for about three months before returning home. During that time, this gracious, older woman encouraged her younger friend and relative. We are confident that Mary felt nourished and refreshed after her visit.

Years later Elizabeth's son, John the Baptist, told those who came to hear him preach, "I baptize you with water. But one more powerful than I will come, the thongs of whose sandals I am not worthy to untie. He will baptize you with the Holy Spirit and with fire" (Luke 3:16).

After Jesus began His public ministry, the crowds started flocking to hear Him. Some of John's followers wondered what was happening, but John explained that this was who he had been waiting for. He had done the job he had been commissioned to do. He responded, "That joy is mine, and it is now complete. He [Jesus] must become greater; I must become less" (John 3:29-30). John was not going to throw a monkey wrench into God's work by demanding attention and success for himself. When he was thrown into prison and became discouraged, Jesus lifted his spirits by telling his messengers, "Go back and report to John what you have seen and heard: The blind receive sight, the lame walk, those who have leprosy are cured, the deaf hear, the dead are raised, and the good news is preached to the poor. Blessed is the man who does not fall away on account of me" (Luke 7:22-23).

Jesus did not rebuke John for the doubts and questions rising in his mind. John had been cut off from active involvement in his previously successful ministry. Sitting alone in that prison he needed affirmation, and Jesus gave it to him. He told John the reassuring facts: Jesus, indeed, was the Messiah, and He was doing the very things the Old Testament had predicted He would do. Jesus didn't rashly promise that John would be released; He knew that wouldn't be. But He quietly spoke words of encouragement: "Don't give up, John. Keep your confidence alive. God is still at work" [our paraphrase].

After John's messengers left, Jesus further supported John as He turned to the crowds. "What did you go out into the desert to see? . . . A prophet? Yes, I tell you, and more than a prophet. This is the one about whom it is written: 'I will send my messenger ahead of you, who will prepare your way before you.' I tell you, among those born of women there is no one greater than John" (Luke 7:24-28). Jesus connected John to the Old Testament prophecy about him. He validated John's work, message, and person.

THINK IT THROUGH

Read again the following biblical illustrations: Jonathan and David (1 Samuel 20), Barnabas and Saul (Acts 9:19-30; 11:19-26), and Elizabeth and Mary (Luke 1:42-56). How can you follow their examples by giving specific encouragement to a friend, relative, or fellow church member?

SOMETHING TO DO

Think of words of encouragement you can offer a friend. Take your pen and write a note today, or pick up the phone and make a call.

4

Destructive Words

The Lord detests lying lips, but he delights in men who are truthful. (Proverbs 12:22)

"A lie is halfway around the world before the truth has a chance to get its shoes on." Thus said a spokesman for Commonwealth Edison in Chicago when a large section of the city lost its electrical power. He was on the radio trying to calm people's fears before total panic erupted.

We heard a host on a radio talk show say, "Aren't rumors fun? They really liven up a show." The phone lines were active as people talked about what they had just heard or speculated about the rumor being discussed.

Winnie recalls that rumors kept life interesting for the prisoners of war interned in China during World War II. They floated by on a daily basis. An offhand comment made by a Chinese coolie bringing in food supplies to the internees would rapidly develop into a rumor. Sometimes a solid piece of news was embellished as it made its rounds through the camp. Speculations about the progress of the war and what was going on outside those guarded walls were always stimulating topics of conversation.

In similar fashion Chuck recalls that rumors were prevalent in his army life. They added spice to the talk in the latrine. Whether the story being circulated at the moment were true or not was usually not of prime concern to either the teller or the hearer. It was passed on because it was titillating or alarming.

We spoke with the assistant manager of purchasing in a local supermarket about the gossip papers, or "rag sheets," that the store sells each week. That particular store made available three or four such publications, and the manager said, "We always sell out our supply of those papers." People seem to have an insatiable desire to read the low-down dirt on others, especially on the rich and famous. Exposé books about celebrities rapidly become best-sellers. One potential author was recently turned down by a publisher because his autobiography didn't have enough interesting revelations.

Christians are not immune to the desire to pass along or listen to choice tidbits. There is something immensely satisfying in saying, "Have you heard this?" and being the first person to communicate the information to the listener. The writer of the Proverbs understood this kind of perverse pleasure, for he wrote, "The words of a gossip are like choice morsels; they go down to a man's inmost parts" (18:8).

Gossip is tasty. Once it is ingested, it lives on in the person who receives it. Even if the rumor is later proved to be untrue, it is difficult to erase the original impression. You may remember personally having to correct an impression because gossip had painted an incorrect picture. We may think rumors and gossip are simply entertaining, but the effects can be devastating and dangerous.

The director of a struggling Bible training school wrote to us that enrollment had dropped because "some malicious individual circulated the false report that we were closing our doors!" Such rumors are insidious because they are so hard to track down and correct. It's like trying to catch falling leaves whipping around in a brisk autumn wind.

We have listened to people tell us interesting, even bizarre, things they have heard about us. A man visited us from

Australia and repeated a piece of gossip he had heard about us when he was elsewhere in the States. The people spreading the "fact" had had no contact with us, yet they were passing it along with "sober concern" as gospel truth. Until our visitor came to us, no one had ever contacted us to substantiate the story.

What is gossip and slander? William Barclay in his *Letter to the Romans* says this:

> *Whisperers* and *slanderers (psithuristes* and *katalalos)*. These two words describe people with slanderous tongues. But there is a difference between them. *Katalalos,* slanderer, quite openly makes his accusations and tells his tales; but *psithuristes* describes the man who whispers his malicious stories in the listener's ears, who will take a man apart into a corner and whisper a character-destroying story. Both are bad, but the whisperer is the worse. A man can at least defend himself against an open slander, but he is helpless against the secret whisperer who delights in destroying reputations.[1]

In our experience a gossip is a person who reveals intimate, personal, sensational, or rumored facts about other individuals, regardless of whether the claims are true.

Why do people engage in gossip?

1. It is an easy way to make conversation.

2. It can be a defense mechanism. If we can draw attention to someone else, then we can avoid revealing anything personal about ourselves. However, a person who is a habitual gossip actually reveals a great deal about himself. The things that fill our minds are what come out of our mouths.

3. It may be a form of self-promotion. It can engender the attitude that "I may not be perfect, but I certainly wouldn't do what So-and-so does." The elder brother displayed that attitude in Christ's story about the prodigal son. Notice how the elder brother compared himself to the returned prodigal. "Look! All these years I've been slaving for you and never disobeyed your orders. Yet you never gave me even a young

1. William Barclay, *Letter to the Romans* (Philadelphia: Westminster, 1957), p. 29.

goat so I could celebrate with my friends. But when this son of yours who has squandered your property with prostitutes comes home, you kill the fattened calf for him!" (Luke 15:29-30).

The older brother's statements about the prodigal's former life-style were true. But his purpose was to promote himself as the better son and also as the injured party. In his mind, his father hadn't shown him such favors. His resentment, anger, and hostility literally bubbled out of his mouth as he pointed his finger at his brother.

4. Gossip gives a sense of importance, of being "in the know."

5. Gossip is a great indoor sport. We enjoy shooting down the high and mighty and puncturing someone else's balloon. Again, if a successful or prominent person reveals that he has feet of clay, we feel better about ourselves.

6. Gossip gives some people a chance to dump their garbage on others. Some husbands and wives feel better after unloading their complaints about their spouses on someone else. The same is true of members of a congregation spouting off about their pastor.

7. It can be a power play, a struggle for control.

8. It can be a cover-up for hidden motives. Let's look more closely at how gossip functions as a cover-up. The facts shared may be couched in such terms as "I'm really concerned about So-and-so." That phrase can become a catch-all for many conflicting emotions. Although it sounds reasonable and spiritual, it can mask such feelings as:

I'm threatened by what that person is doing.
I don't want to make any changes in my thinking or actions.
I don't want to confront that issue.
I'm upset because he is rocking the boat.
I felt put down by what he said/did.
I'm angry because I was ignored.
I really don't like that person.
Why should we listen to someone so young?

"SHE BLASTS PEOPLE, THEN EXCUSES HERSELF BY SAYING, 'I CAN'T HELP BEING BRUTALLY FRANK.' FRANKLY, I THINK SHE'S JUST BRUTAL."

Who does he think he is, coming in here telling us what to do?

I know just as much, if not more, than that person, yet no one is asking my opinion.

Those are often the emotions that are covered up. Unfortunately, they often surface in prayer meetings, committee meetings, or deacons' meetings. Places where we are supposedly doing God's work often end up being the places where God's people are most viciously torn down.

Romans 1:29-31 accurately describes how mankind looks to God: "They [men and women] have become filled with every kind of wickedness, evil, greed and depravity. They are full of envy, murder, strife, deceit and malice. They are gossips, slanderers, God-haters, insolent, arrogant and boastful; they invent ways of doing evil; they disobey their parents; they are senseless, faithless, heartless, ruthless." It is difficult and embarrassing to read those words. Too often we see these qualities in ourselves and those characteristics reflected in our words.

Has it always been this way? In the next chapter we look back to the beginning when God enjoyed intimate fellowship with His highest creation.

THINK IT THROUGH

Give sober attention to Psalm 55:21 and Proverbs 4:23-24.

The answers to situations that may provoke us to use evil words can be found in Psalm 19:14; 141:3.

SOMETHING TO DO

Write out Psalm 141:3, and place it near your phone or on the dashboard of your car.

5

Our Beginning

The Lord blesses his people with peace. (Psalm 29:11)

Chuck loves to fish. He likes to catch them, but if they aren't biting, he still enjoys the peace and tranquillity of the lake. We frequently vacation on a lake in the north woods of Minnesota—far away from traffic, pollution, and telephones. There is something soothing about water that perfectly mirrors the trees on the shore. We have scores of slides with such mirror-images taken over the course of many years, reflecting how much we as urban people value peace and quiet.

However, the lake is not always perfectly serene. When the wind blows, the stillness is disrupted. To apply the analogy, when God created the first man and woman, they were to reflect His image—His person and His character. And in the initial serenity and peace of the Garden, His plan was carried out. But then an ill wind blew in to distort that reflection. The result was dissension and separation.

Adam and Eve were created in the image of God. God used Himself as the pattern for handcrafting them. That made them distinct from the rest of creation. In reflecting God's person Adam and Eve communicated verbally with God. They were able to think and make decisions. They expressed emotions, such as love, compassion, faithfulness, commitment. They worshiped and glorified God. They would be eternal beings as God was eternal—a foundational truth that gives dignity to all human beings but is almost impossible to grasp.

God did not create human beings to live in isolation from one another. He created Adam and Eve for relationship—relationship with Himself and with each other. Their interaction with each other would reflect partnership, cooperation, and common goals.

God created two whole individuals to work together in harmony to achieve goals and to find fulfillment in life. And all the while they were to enjoy God and each other. The picture was one of beautiful, idyllic wholeness.

Sadly, the story didn't continue with "and they lived happily ever after." Sin brought "holes" into that complete environment, and there have been problems ever since. The perfect reflection of God's person and activity became distorted.

Sin is not a popular word in our vocabulary. In fact, it is seldom used. We say people are "victims of their circumstances," or they "make mistakes." The Bible, however, does not waffle on this issue. Sin is recognized for what it is: rebellion against God.

In spite of all their advantages, Adam and Eve chose to rebel against God's authority. They disobeyed His explicit instructions, creating a big "hole" in the Garden of Eden, the results of which have affected us ever since.

When the serpent tempted them, he insinuated that God was cheating them by denying them the fruit of the one restricted tree. He appealed to their self-interest by saying, "You will be like God." It is no wonder that self-interest and pride motivate people's lives today.

After they had eaten the fruit, Adam and Eve felt inadequate and ashamed and tried to cover themselves with fig leaves. Their relationship with God broke down. When they heard God coming, they hid. The holes of guilt, shame, lowered self-esteem, and fear appeared.

Their relationship with each other deteriorated as well. Adam pointed the finger of blame at his wife. Eve pointed at the serpent. Even though that marriage literally had been made in heaven, hostility, resentment, and accusations began to surface. Great defects marred their wholeness and shattered the reflection. It wasn't long before violence and murder entered that first home.

The great beginning was sadly disfigured, but it was not left to self-destruct. God intervened to produce a new creation through faith, through a Redeemer, the Lord Jesus Christ. He promised a Redeemer to Adam and Eve and all their descendants. By faith in Jesus Christ their shattered lives could be recreated to once again reflect the image of God (Romans 8:29).

We have seen restless, fearful people become serene, confident individuals after placing their faith in Christ. We

IT'S NOT MY FAULT!"

have also seen frantically ambitious business people discover meaning and purpose in hard work because of Him. Christ provides fulfillment and joy in doing one's job well and promises forgiveness if we have faith. The knowledge that every individual was created by God Himself helped a young woman to find healing and wholeness for her fractured life.

Sara (not her real name) was a middle child born into a religious, church-going family. For some reason, her parents rejected her. From earliest childhood she was kept locked alone in the basement. Her older and younger siblings were apparently treated normally, but Sara was fed leftovers from the table. Her parents gave her hand-me-downs and never purchased new clothes for her.

The only time she was allowed out of the basement was when the family went to church on Sunday. During the long hours she spent alone in the basement throughout the week she would think about what she had learned in Sunday school, and she would talk to Jesus. When she was old enough to go to school, she was let out, but otherwise, she lived a life cut off from the rest of her family. She grew up thinking she deserved their awful treatment and that she was a terrible person.

When she finally left home and went away to a Christian college, she learned that God had created her as an individual. She began to study the attributes of God in the Bible on her own. She would say to herself, "This is the pattern God used to make me." The more she learned about God, the more she learned to accept the person God had created her to be.

It wasn't easy for her to forgive her parents for what they had done to her. After a long struggle, Sara finally flew home one day to tell her parents, "I forgive you." As far as we know, they have never asked Sara for her forgiveness or admitted their wrongdoing. Yet Sara was able to say, "For the first time in years, I felt free. I went out and bought myself a ring to celebrate!"

Sara had invited Christ into her life as a child. She is sure that is why she didn't totally lose her mind. Although she has not fully recovered from the emotional damage, the realization that God created her allowed her to begin the process of regaining the dignity and personhood that had been taken from her.

Every human being can trace his or her roots back to God's creation. Male or female, we are created in the image of God. That is what gives such force to James' statement: "With the tongue we praise our Lord and Father, and with it we curse man, *who have been made in God's likeness*" (James 3:9; italics added).

THINK IT THROUGH

Think about your roots. How does being created in the image of God affect your attitude about yourself? As you reflect on your past and present, think of people who have been created by the Lord and are living out the characteristics of God. Give thanks for them. Read Ephesians 1:15-16.

Think about those who have suffered the marring of sin in their lives and who now need God's forgiveness and your forgiveness, as well as words of encouragement. Read the following Scriptures for examples: Luke 15:11-24; 18:9-14; John 4:7-29.

In what ways are you reflecting Jesus Christ in your life?

SOMETHING TO DO

Begin to pray regularly for someone who is out of sorts with people and out of fellowship with God. Look for the Lord's working in that person's life. What can you do to encourage a reversal in his or her thinking and actions?

6

Our Failings

A gossip separates close friends. (Proverbs 16:28)

"Our church is being torn apart by gossip. People seem more interested in meeting their own agendas than in thinking about what is best for the congregation," commented a pastor.

Satan uses gossip to tear local churches apart. When we criticize, agitate, and express anger behind people's backs, we are cooperating with his plans. He would like to see all local churches immobilized. If gossip and bickering will accomplish that, then that's the approach he will use. Why do the people who have been created in the image of God and redeemed by Jesus Christ still let such ill winds blow through their lives and distort the image of the Savior, whom they should be reflecting?

We have seen bewilderment, anger, frustration, even despair on the part of leaders who feel like they are struggling in an uphill journey where the end never seems to be in sight. Too many people born into the family of God have not grown. Paul wrote about Christians who still drank milk when they should have been eating meat. He was referring to "carnal Christians"—people easily influenced by the world around them. Such Christians sometimes engage in spiritual battles only to suffer critical losses.

Living the Christian life is a process. The believer who actively strives to follow and obey Jesus Christ will more and more accurately reflect His image. The Christian who chooses to go his own way will mar the reflection and in its place wreak destruction.

For what reason do people attack one another through gossip, backbiting, criticism, and even slander? What motivates hostility among Christians, churches, and Christian organizations? Why haven't God's children matured beyond such behavior? We have uncovered the following reasons.

1. *Refusal to submit to authority.* It's amazing how often that is mentioned as a source of dissension. Men who accept the authority of their boss at work refuse to recognize authority in the church. Men who are managers at work sometimes carry a dictatorial attitude into the church. Women who are successful in professional careers sometimes find it hard to yield to church leadership.

"He (she) never accepts anyone's authority" is a comment we have heard many times. That is a serious character flaw, especially in people who claim to be followers of Jesus Christ. As we have discussed, the problem dates back to the Garden of Eden, but Christ came to reveal a better way. Although Jesus was equal with God, He voluntarily yielded to the leadership of His heavenly Father. Even more remarkable, Jesus, the Creator, submitted to the authority of His own creation—His earthly parents (cf. Luke 2:51).

In our democratic society, every individual is regarded as important, but the decisions of government are made by an elected few. If everyone did exactly as he or she pleased, there would be chaos. Of course, our leaders are not always right. If they make foolish decisions, we can vote them out of office. But while they are in office we abide by the laws they establish. We accept the authority of our secular government; why do we have such a hard time accepting leadership in the church?

Church leaders are not perfect; few would claim to be. And unfortunately, the public exposure of some who completely fail is discouraging. It is true that some leaders in the church have abused authority, but they are really the exception to the norm. And there are better ways of handling disappointment with authorities than starting a whispering campaign against the pastor or Sunday school superintendent.

2. *Fear of change.* A significant source of gossip among Christians is the refusal to accept change. The older generation in a church is not the only one subject to this fear; younger people may also avoid change for different reasons.

We are referring to method and traditions, not doctrine. Jesus took a hard line on unthinking traditions. The religious legalists of His day criticized Jesus and His disciples for not observing all the ceremonial rules. Jesus responded by quoting from the Old Testament: "These people honor me with their lips, but their hearts are far from me. They worship me in vain; their teachings are but rules taught by men" (Mark 7:6-7; cf. Isaiah 29:13). Fear of change is not a valid reason to initiate conflict.

Through the years we have had the opportunity to associate with other Christians in a wide variety of churches. Worship styles range from informal to highly structured. People develop a sense of security when they know what to expect. Introduce a change in the times of worship, length of service, order of hymns and prayer, style of music—almost any deviation from the norm guarantees an emotional response. Order of worship in a local church, however it may be done, becomes so sacred to some people that any variation is viewed as heresy. We have heard some angry attacks leveled at people who introduced change.

Yet Jesus Himself brought about drastic changes. He desired hearts that were committed to Him, not rituals. He valued worship that came from the heart in love and faith and devotion.

Specific formats in worship are not divinely inspired. It is unfortunate that God's people tend to lock Him into rituals. Sometimes He has to forcibly shake them out of the ruts they

"YOU CAN PREACH AS LONG AS YOU LIKE, YOUNG MAN,
BUT THE TRADITION AT OUR CHURCH IS THAT NOBODY
EVER GETS SAVED AFTER 12 O'CLOCK."

try to prescribe for Him. We don't wish the trauma of disaster on anyone but we encourage those who rigidly think, *God cannot bless us unless we do it this way,* to be more flexible.

James said, "Everyone should be quick to listen, slow to speak and slow to become angry, for man's anger does not bring about the righteous life that God desires" (1:19-20).

3. *Selfishness and pride.* Christians who are supposedly growing often refuse to let go of self-centeredness, independence, and arrogance.

"I'll do that if I feel like it."

"I don't feel like it, so I won't do it."

"No one is going to tell me what I should or should not be doing."

"I have put in my time for years. Let the younger ones assume some of the responsibility."

"Don't ask me to sacrifice my time. It's mine!"

"This is a free country, and I can do as I wish."

Sometimes we make excuses to cover our attitude that "that job is beneath me." We do not like to relinquish our pride.

The most disruptive factor of a selfish attitude is that people don't keep their word. If something more interesting comes along, they just don't show up for whatever they had agreed to do. Then if someone else reminds them of their commitment, they accuse that person of putting undue pressure on them.

Sometimes we selfishly refuse to commit ourselves to responsibility. If a church commitment infringes on our right to freedom, we either rationalize our way out of it or criticize the person who "coerced" us into making the commitment in the first place.

Winnie's school in China was British. She was taught that nothing was as binding as "the word of an Englishman." People did not sign contracts. Their word was sufficient. The Bible says, "Simply let your 'Yes' be 'Yes,' and your 'No,' 'No'" (Matthew 5:37).

The psalmist commends the person "who keeps his oath [his word] even when it hurts" (Psalm 15:4*b*).

4. *Insecurity*. Feelings of inadequacy are never an excuse to claim, "My most important priority is to feel good about myself." However, it is important to note that insecurity is sometimes the cause of feelings of jealousy and anger.

People feel threatened when someone else comes along with an equal or greater gift. For example, a Sunday school teacher has taught the three- and four-year-olds for years. She loves it—it's her niche. But someone younger comes along with the same kind of love and enthusiasm for teaching children. The older teacher feels threatened. That is her domain. So she begins to make critical comments about this younger person to other people. Perhaps she makes offhand remarks to the parents of children in the class.

That can go both ways. The new teacher may criticize the more experienced one with such asides as, "She's probably in a rut after teaching all these years," or, "Do you know if Mrs. So-and-so has gone to a Sunday school conference recently to get some fresh ideas?" Casting aspersion on someone else's ability or character can be developed into a creative verbal art. Unfortunately, Christians sometimes become masters at this art to cover their own sense of inadequacy.

Some people withdraw in their insecurity. Silence and withdrawal can communicate nonverbalized anger.

5. *Excessive commitment to a cause.* Some people can become contentious because they really care about an issue. They let their emotions override their self-control. The problem arises when we keep trying to fight the battle after a decision has been made. It is OK to express concerns, as long as it is done graciously. However, once a decision has been made, we need to learn to accept it and move on. When we refuse to let matters rest, we open the door for gossip to gain a foothold.

On one occasion a Christian organization that we cared about deeply was making a decision that we believed was not in its best interest, or God's. We expressed our concern with a great deal of passion. The person receiving the message understood us, but it didn't alter the decision. We had to let the matter drop.

In contrast to contentions within the church, Jesus said, "By this all men will know that you are my disciples, if you love one another" (John 13:35).

THINK IT THROUGH

Describe the attitudes and words that create problems among God's people in the following Scriptures. What action solved the problem and prevented God's judgment? Read Numbers 14:1-20; Nehemiah 5:1-13; Acts 6:1-6.

SOMETHING TO DO

Think of a problem your church faces that needs correction. Do the above Scriptures give clues to solutions? Can you do something to help? Think about volunteering your help, if appropriate. If not, pray about it.

7

How Our Culture
Shapes Our Words

Do not conform any longer to the pattern of this world.
(Romans 12:2)

People love to talk. Listen to teens on a crowded bus and
to fishermen lounging on a dock with cups of coffee. Social
exchange continues from generation to generation. But always
conversation indicates a great deal about the society in which
we live.

The conversations of cultures reflect deep-seated ideas
and mores. The actual words may be about love, business,
comfort, or justice, but they communicate whatever underlying anger, deceit, honesty, or contentment is prevalent in society at that time and place.

Paul called the Christian to be made new in the attitudes
of the mind, in contrast to unbelievers who are futile in their
thinking and darkened in their understanding (see Romans
12:2; Ephesians 4:17). That newness of mind and heart will
reflect the wisdom of God and will countermand shallow
thinking and speech in our society. However, there are three

cultural values that continue to be widely reflected in our thoughtless speech.

The crowning essence of the American way seems to be the *rights* of the individual. In our Constitution we claim inalienable rights to life, liberty, and the pursuit of happiness. "We're equal—don't rob me of my privileges," we state emphatically. These concerns seem to be a primary raison d'être for life in the American culture, if not for Western civilization as a whole. We struggle, talk, argue, and protest in response to any diminution of our rights. Because we regard them as necessary to survival, we take every opportunity to ridicule any idea that would limit us. "Gather a support group! Cut down the opposition! Maintain our rights at all costs!" we cry.

Another significant way in which our attitudes and speech mirror society is through our *entertainment models.* Because personalities are highly visible in the mass media, our heroes' lives influence the way we think and act. Although the media influences thousands, announcers and talk show hosts pretend great intimacy. Intimacy and friendliness characterize the deejay and the program host. We listen to their chatter, their observations about life, their gossip. We readily accept the comedian or news reporter who talks about others. Unconsciously, we pick up the thoughtless habit of discussing those distant heroes, their foibles, and their escapades. We carelessly enjoy so many vicarious experiences that when we encounter the concrete incidents of real friends around us, we are blasé and crass. We seem to mix fantasy and reality and then laugh it all off as if nothing mattered at all.

How do Americans survive in our society with all of its clashing ideas and energy? Through the third cultural value reflected in our speech—*competition.* Our goal is to win, to sell more than anyone else, to make the largest profit, to climb to the top. It's the American way. Sports would go nowhere without that competitive drive. One sports columnist summed up this attitude when he said, "The only important statistic [for a great quarterback] is winning."[1] The person who fights

1. Don Pierson, "He Won't Tell You, But Montana's No. 1," *Chicago Tribune,* 9 November 1989.

harder, works longer hours, and is more creative or clever achieves the goal.

Competition in our culture also displays itself in the political arena. Our election process thrives on words and negotiations. A strategy for a new campaign is always simmering. That's how politics go, we say. Opposition within the political party would seem to be a reasonable concept, but too often when we start talking, loyalty is set aside, and destructive suspicions begin to characterize relationships. A whispering campaign may be the way to keep the fires going.

The spirit of competition is not left on the playing field or in politics, however; it ranges about in our personal lives. With our words we try to outdo even good friends simply because we love to beat out anyone who appears to be ahead of us. The rancor and shady negotiations of politics even cripple the effectiveness of the Christian church.

God didn't create Adam and Eve to compete with each other. He created them to complement one another in a harmonious, cooperative relationship. "Should you then seek great things for yourself? Seek them not" (Jeremiah 45:5).

Is competition wrong then? Not necessarily. The Bible acknowledges that the winner in a race receives the prize. There is a place for healthy competition. However, in the Christian life we are not to compete with one another with intent to outdo each other. Instead, we compete against ourselves. The Bible says, "Let us run with perseverance the race *marked out for us*" (Hebrews 12:1*b*; italics added).

In the body of believers tasks are marked out for each person. If every believer functioned as a spiritually healthy member of the body, Christians wouldn't be elbowing one another out of the way. There's room for everyone to function together, but these attitudes must go:

"We must get ahead no matter what it takes."

"Let's beat that church down the road in our attendance at Vacation Bible School."

"The reality is this is a dog-eat-dog world, so we do what we have to do."

"Stepping on a few people to get there is just the price you pay."

You can probably think of many other clichés that depict the competitive attitude in society that has infected the church.

Husbands and wives compete with each other. Parents compete with children, brothers with sisters. Individuals in a church compete to be recognized; churches compete with each other to be acknowledged in the community. Christian organizations compete for recognition, power, influence, the profit bottom-line.

Where is the cooperation among God's people that He intended? Why don't we acknowledge, "Your place and your effort are just as important as mine. How can I help and support you to become all that God has created and redeemed you to be?"

The brutal aspects of a competitive spirit is another glaring hole that appeared after sin entered. Cain was determined to be recognized and accepted, even if he had to step on his brother's body to do it.

A driving, competitive attitude can cause Christians to be equally irrational. People will attack their brothers and sisters in Christ in speech rather than look at themselves to see if they are the ones who should change. When we attack other believers, we ultimately hurt ourselves because we are all members of the same body.

In running the race marked out for him, Paul kept his focus where it belonged—on the Person of Jesus Christ. By its very nature competition forces us to focus on other people and on what they are doing. So we strive against each other. In contrast, the scriptural pattern is this:

> Let us throw off everything that hinders and the sin that so easily entangles, and let us run with perseverance the race marked out for us. Let us fix our eyes on Jesus, the author and perfecter of our faith, who for the joy set before him endured the cross, scorning its shame, and sat down at the right hand of the throne of God. Consider him who endured such opposition

from sinful men, so that you will not grow weary and lose heart. (Hebrews 12:1-3)

We can't escape our culture, but we can think about it and consciously attempt to be like the Lord Jesus was in His society—a gracious speaker. That should be the goal for each one of us.

THINK IT THROUGH

New Testament writers warn their readers about the influence of the world around us. Study these verses: Romans 12:1-2; James 4:13-17; 1 Peter 2:9-12; 1 John 2:15-17.

SOMETHING TO DO

We need to exercise discipline over the negative influences in our lives. Determine what influences are affecting your life now, and then take control of them. Do you participate in unsavory conversations at work? Do you watch unwholesome television programs? Read certain magazines? Is your life-style determined by those influences?

8

Learning a New Language

Let your conversation be always full of grace.
(Colossians 4:6)

Following a Sunday morning service, Winnie was talking with an international student who was studying at an evangelical seminary in the States. Winnie mentioned that we were working on this book, and the student asked what kind of emphasis we were giving it.

"Right now," Winnie replied, "we're zeroing in on the area of gossip. It's tough. For example, this week I encountered a fresh aspect of gossip. I work part-time as a nurse in a doctor's office, and many families from our local church come to that office for their medical care. We have had a measles epidemic in our congregation even though most of the children have already been immunized against the disease. Consequently, many of the parents brought their children to be re-immunized. At work I gave shots to families I know, and in discussing the unusual epidemic with another member of the congregation I almost said, 'Oh, the Barker family was in the office last night for their injections,' but I caught myself and didn't mention it."

"Doctors and nurses are trained to maintain confidentiality," she continued. "That would not have been considered a major breach of confidence, but what went through my mind at that moment was, 'It is neither my business nor my privilege to pass on this information.' The parents themselves could relate that information. It was their prerogative to do so, not mine. The only benefit I would have gained in the telling would have been to communicate to my friend that 'Winnie knows something you don't.' This whole subject of gossip," Winnie concluded, "has made me far more conscious of what I am saying. I ask myself, Why am I saying this? And how will this information be perceived by the hearer?"

The overseas student exclaimed, "That's just like learning a new language! Before I speak, I have to ask myself, what is the right word in English? What does it mean? And in this context how will the person I am talking to understand or perceive it?" That particular young woman from Germany speaks fluent Spanish, and her command of English is outstanding. In two years' time in this country she has learned many of the idioms of our language and converses in American English with great ease. Yet her ability to do so has taken both mental and verbal discipline.

God speaks a different language than we do, and we're not talking about Greek, Hebrew, Chinese, German, or English. Instead, God's language expresses who He is. His words reveal His character—holy, true, pure, right, just, reliable, loving. That produces constant tension for His hearers because we are anything but perfect.

Jesus Christ bridged the language barrier between God and man. He was the most effective communicator of all time, yet He had to ask His listeners, "Why is my language not clear to you?" (John 8:43*a*).

Jesus had been teaching about truth and freedom, challenging His audience's definitions of those terms. He explained God's definitions and showed the people how their thinking was not in line with God's. Then He answered His own question.

"You know, Dad, this thinking before I talk is like learning to speak a new language!"

Because you are unable to hear what I say. You belong to your father, the devil, and you want to carry out your father's desire. He was a murderer from the beginning, not holding to the truth, for there is no truth in him. When he lies, he speaks his native language, for he is a liar and the father of lies. . . . He who belongs to God hears what God says. The reason you do not hear is that you do not belong to God. (John 8:43*b*-47)

Their words revealed to whom they belonged. It was strong teaching, and His audience didn't like it. Their response was to try to stone Jesus (v. 59). Their words and actions proved the point Jesus was making: they didn't belong to God. And if they didn't belong to God, then they still belonged to Satan and were under his control.

The Greek term for "devil" in John 8:44 is *diablos*. It means slanderous or accusing falsely and is used many times throughout the New Testament to refer to the devil. The same term is also translated as "malicious gossips," "malicious talkers," or "slanderers." Paul, writing to Timothy, warned, "But mark this: There will be terrible times in the last days. People will be lovers of themselves, lovers of money, boastful, proud, abusive, disobedient to their parents, ungrateful, unholy, without love, unforgiving, slanderous [*diablos*], without self-control, brutal, not lovers of the good, treacherous, rash, conceited, lovers of pleasure rather than lovers of God—having a form of godliness but denying its power" (2 Timothy 3:1-5). As in the days when Jesus lived on earth, so it will be when He comes again.

People's language and actions depict ownership. They belong to God or to the devil. That classification isn't any easier for us to accept now than it was centuries ago when the Lord first spoke those words.

We need a new ownership. The first step is getting transferred from Satan's domain to God's. We need to learn a new language. To learn God's language we have to be born, or adopted, into God's family. The transaction is accomplished when we place personal faith in Jesus Christ. Having established that relationship with Christ, the second step is to discard the old speech habits like ragged clothing and replace them with the new language that reflects God's character. The apostle Paul described it this way:

> Put off your old self . . . and . . . put on the new self, created to be like God in true righteousness and holiness. Therefore each of you must put off falsehood and speak truthfully. . . . "In your anger do not sin": Do not let the sun go down while you are still angry, and do not give the devil a foothold. . . . Do not let any unwholesome talk come out of your mouths, but only what is helpful for building others up. . . . Get rid of all bitterness, rage and anger, brawling and slander, along with every form of malice. Be kind and compassionate to one another, forgiving each other, just as in Christ God forgave you. (Ephesians 4:22-32)

We learn language as babies in the context of the family relationship. When we are born into God's family through faith in Jesus Christ, a new relationship is established. The Bible says, "If anyone is in Christ, he is a new creation; the old has gone, the new has come!" (2 Corinthians 5:17).

When each of our three grandchildren was born, a family relationship was established. As that relationship develops, one of the exciting features is teaching the children to use words. The baby coos and gurgles. The three-year-old and the five-year-old are continuously increasing their communications skills.

As their vocabularies grow, they move to the second stage of learning to discard and replace. When our own children were young, we did not allow them to say "shut up." Because it was prohibited, it became appealing to one of our sons. Winnie caught him one day when he was about five years old, crouched behind the sofa saying, "Shut up, shut up, shut up." He was relishing a prohibited, tasty morsel, for he had not yet learned to discard the words that had no place in our relationship.

Through the years as we have seen people enter into relationships with Jesus Christ, we have often noted a marked transformation between the "old" and "new" speech patterns. One woman said she used to have "a mouth like a truck driver's." After Christ came into her life, her language was one of the first areas to be transformed. For a while, her family thought they had a stranger living in their house. Gradually, each of them came to know Jesus, and they all clearly understood that with a new creation came a new language. God calls Christians to help one another grow in learning that language.

Peter was one of Jesus' disciples who had a hard time controlling his tongue. He didn't do things halfway. His intense enthusiasm and energy made his mistakes glaringly obvious. But his growth in the area of speech is an encouragement to all of us. In his second letter he laid down sound principles that we can apply to the concept of learning a new language.

"SHUT UP! SHUT UP! SHUT UP!"

THINK IT THROUGH

How would you describe your words and your conversation? Read Ecclesiastes 10:12. Do you talk about God, His Word, and His concerns? (Psalm 34:1). Or does another kind of language come out of your mouth? See James 3:14.

SOMETHING TO DO

Have you ever established a regular Bible reading time? Read Matthew 4:4 and Joshua 1:8. Has the time set for your devotions somehow evaporated? Begin again. Ask for forgiveness, and start reading a chapter a day. Try starting with the book of Mark. We will never use God's language unless we are exposed to it.

9

Jesus the Listener

Let the wise listen and add to their learning. (Proverbs 1:5)

Jesus Christ is called the Word—an appropriate metaphor. God spoke, and the universe came into being. The three Persons of the Godhead communicate with each other (Genesis 1:26). Throughout the New Testament the Son speaks to the Father, and the Father to the Son. The Holy Spirit teaches and endorses what has been said (John 14:26; 15:26). Jesus Christ embodied God's final message to mankind (Hebrews 1:1-3).

How would you describe Jesus' speech? Take a few minutes and think about everything you have heard about Jesus' words. Write down your observations before reading any further.

We asked that question at a family conference, and these were the responses:

Authoritative	Compassionate
Gentle	Direct
Wise	Tactful
Knowledgeable	Truthful

Simple	Challenging
Humble	Obedient
Unselfish	Life-giving
Loving	

Children and ordinary people understood His words. Everyone marveled at His gracious speech. They were challenged by the authority with which He spoke. His speech revealed His character.

Jesus' questions revealed His willingness to listen. The disciples sometimes wanted to push people away. They impatiently considered the Canaanite woman from Tyre and Sidon a nuisance. But Jesus listened to her and met her need (Matthew 15:21-28).

Jesus responded similarly to a blind man who called to Him in an incident recorded in Mark 10:46-52. He listened to the woman who had determined to get near Him to touch His cloak (Mark 5:24-34). Maybe the critical disciples thought that such people would discredit their "movement."

What if Jesus had passed by Samaria as His disciples preferred? Their racial prejudice was typical of that area, but we would have missed the wonderful encounter between Jesus and the woman at the well. He listened to her and gave her the answers for which she had been searching all her life.

Jesus' habit of listening was developed early in life. At the age of twelve He was found sitting in the Temple among the teachers *"listening* to them and asking them questions" (Luke 2:46; italics added). Everyone was amazed at the depth of His comprehension.

He also listened to His earthly parents. In Luke 2:51 we read that He "was obedient to them." At the end of His life He said to His disciples, "Everything that I learned from my Father I have made known to you" (John 15:15).

Jesus had a good example of listening in His own home because Mary, His mother, was a listener. She thought about the things she heard (Luke 2:51). Her Magnificat in Luke 1:46-55 reveals that she had absorbed a great deal of the Old Testament as a young girl. She must have paid attention when the Scriptures were read in the synagogue or in her home, perhaps in accordance with Deuteronomy 6:4-9. The concepts of God and His sovereign work in Israel's history had engaged her mind, and she verbalized what she had learned in that beautiful song of praise.

Apparently, Mary also learned to listen to her son Jesus. When a crisis arose at the wedding at Cana, she told Jesus about the problem and then calmly said to the servants, "Do whatever he tells you" (John 2:5). She had learned that whatever Jesus said was worth listening to and acting upon. Jesus' words in verse 4 also indicate that Mary understood something about His mission and purpose in life.

A person beginning to learn a new language must listen. His words and actions reveal what he is absorbing. Many times we make inaccurate snap judgments because we have not taken the time to hear and absorb all the facts. We heard an educator being interviewed on the radio who said that in the normal context of life the average person hears 25 percent of what is said and retains only 10 percent of what he hears. We are living proof of that dismal statistic since we can recall the statistic but not the person who said it or occasion or broadcast on which it was said! "Consider carefully what you hear," Jesus admonished (Mark 4:24).

The art of listening is exactly that—an *art*. It is not a skill that most people pick up easily. It has to be developed. Most of us want others to hear what we have to say, but we ourselves are unwilling to listen. In America we rudely begin to talk before the other person is finished. An interrupter is not a listener.

How many times have you been in conversation with someone whose eyes wander around the room to see who else is there? Sometimes we pretend to listen, but that blank look in our eyes betrays us. Perhaps you allow yourself to be easily distracted, or maybe you wait impatiently for the other person to finish so you can tell your story.

Here are a few simple suggestions for learning to listen. Look at the person who is speaking without allowing your eyes or mind to wander. It is important to pay complete attention to what is being said. When we notice the tone of voice and the body language, as well as the words, we show that we attach importance to what is being said—that we really *hear* it. Watch a good mother when she disciplines her child. When the youngster looks right into her eyes, his ear is more likely to listen.

A number of years ago the University of Nebraska's Department of Human and Family Services conducted a survey of strong families in the United States. One of the six strengths those healthy families had in common was good communication. Family members not only talked with each other, but they also knew how to listen and tune in.

Listening to children should be similar to listening to adults. If adults listen to children as they are growing up, those children will be more likely to listen to adults when they are adolescents. When a child is speaking to you, try to stoop

down to the child's level so that you can make eye contact. One of our children tended to speak more slowly and hesitantly than the others, and his siblings often would complete his sentences for him in their impatience. We had to teach the other children patience in listening.

Someone who truly listens shows respect for the speaker. Mutual respect is a missing dimension in our communication today. What if you don't respect the person who is talking? Try to remember that he has been created in the image of God. James points out that we use the same tongue to praise God as we do to curse men. "With the tongue we praise our Lord and Father, and with it we curse men, *who have been made in God's likeness*" (James 3:9; italics added). The real target of our disrespect is God Himself.

A scruffy, unkempt young man wandered into L'Abri in Switzerland one day. Francis Schaeffer shook his hand and greeted him warmly with the words "I'm so glad to meet you."

The young man was startled and said, "You said that like you really meant it."

"I did," replied Dr. Schaeffer.

"How could you?" asked the man. "No one else has ever said he was glad to meet me."

"Because I see in you a person who has been made in the image of God."

If we viewed every individual as a person handcrafted by God, we would treat each with respect. We would probably change how we listen and what we say. James emphasizes this point: "Take note of this: Everyone should be quick to listen, slow to speak" (1:19).

The late Robert J. Little, a superb Bible teacher, used to use this illustration. He said, "Imagine you have two jars on the table. One is filled with honey, the other with vinegar. You accidentally knock both jars over. What comes out of the jars?" The answer was obvious: "What was already inside." Our words—especially those which spill out in quick response to someone else's words or actions—reveal what we have stored up inside.

Jesus is God's Word to us. How much do we listen to Him?

THINK IT THROUGH

How have you practiced the art of listening this past week? Read Psalm 85:8; Proverbs 10:19; James 1:19.

Study the passages in Matthew 15:21-28; Mark 10:46-52; and 5:24-34. Note Jesus' example of listening.

It is quite easy to think of times in life when we haven't listened. Now think of times when you listened, were warned or encouraged, and how blessed you were when you responded.

SOMETHING TO DO

To make progress in your listening, jot down three or four comments your friend, spouse, or child said yesterday. It's hard to remember them, isn't it? Now, concentrate on listening today and write down these comments. Is there a difference in your relationships as a result of your listening? What benefit has this exercise brought?

10

The Power of Words
in the Family

*Listen, my son, to your father's instruction and do not for-
sake your mother's teaching. (Proverbs 1:8)*

Learning to listen and to speak God's language begins in
the home, the place where impressions and discipline make
the strongest impact on children. When a parent talks, an in-
fant's attention follows that familiar voice. A child's comprehension grows. The parent gives simple instructions at first,
and the child responds. He experiments with words, then
phrases, and finally concepts and ideas. In the normal verbal
give-and-take in a home, the child usually develops positive or
negative attitudes in response to what he hears.

Parents teach respect by speaking to their children with
respect. Chuck worked with children for years in church, in
camps, and at a radio station in Chicago. He constantly treated children with respect. (He wouldn't write this about himself, but his wife can.) He didn't talk down to them or belittle
them, and children responded positively. He showed the same
respect to our own children, and the pattern continues with
our grandchildren.

Sometimes, however, children have to learn respect for authority the hard way. When one of our sons was seven, he took a dare to write a note to "Bozo" with some smart remarks and put it on the school principal's windshield. Our son wrote the note and naively signed his name before placing it under the windshield wiper. He and his friends giggled at the fun until the principal went to his car, read the note, and strode across the street to our house. A thoroughly chagrined little boy had to face the principal that day, and he learned a valuable lesson about respect, appropriate speech, and accountability for his words.

Having mutual respect in a family doesn't mean there can't be strong discussions. Our dinner table frequently became an open forum about various issues. We discussed politics, religion, boyfriends, sports, girlfriends, every subject in the school curriculum, sex, prejudice, feminism, and theology. The discussions were animated, sometimes argumentative. Someone was always playing the "devil's advocate"— usually Chuck. Sometimes we had to fight for the floor, but we also learned to listen to one another, to cooperate. We allowed the children to exercise their freedom of speech.

No subject was off limits, unless the conversation degenerated into what we labeled "ninnyolatry," or worship of the immature. That term cropped up frequently, especially in the telling of jokes. We liked to laugh and we enjoyed jokes within limits, but maybe Paul had ninnyolatry in mind when he said, "Do not let any unwholesome talk come out of your mouths" (Ephesians 4:29). We also did not allow swearing and crude language. We told the children that people who have to resort to dirty words reveal their own paucity in vocabulary. We hear Christians use such expressions as "Oh my God!" with alarmingly increasing frequency. It is so easy to carelessly imitate the world about us.

Even in open discussion among family members, derogatory statements about other people should not go unchallenged. It is important for children to learn the difference between attacking an idea or philosophy and attacking the person espousing it. We wanted to build positive attitudes toward other people, and particularly toward fellow Christians. We might have "roast sermon" for Sunday dinner, but we tried not to chew up the preacher. We didn't always succeed, but we tried.

Because such discussions were encouraged in our home, the kids themselves continued them on a more informal basis. Sometimes one of our teenagers would materialize in the bedroom doorway after we had turned off both the light and our minds and say, "Can I ask you a question?" At that time of night there was seldom a simple yes or no answer. Those deep topics rarely came up during planned discussion times. They crept up unexpectedly, usually one-on-one, at odd hours. Those occasions allowed us to make a practice of praying with the children about any issue.

When Moses prepared the people of Israel to enter the Promised Land he said,

> Love the Lord your God with all your heart and with all your soul and with all your strength. These commandments that I give you today are to be upon your hearts. Impress them on your children. Talk about them when you sit at home and when you walk along the road, when you lie down and when you get up. (Deuteronomy 6:5-7)

The parents in the nation of Israel were charged with the responsibility of communicating the facts and principles of God's teaching. They had to learn God's language within the context of the normal activities of everyday life. A parent's life was to reflect a personal relationship with God. For any parent who truly loves God, that is neither duty nor a chore but a privilege.

The family is a microcosm of the world and society. What children learn at home is what they will take with them when they are grown. A woman we know only as Lemuel's mother understood this.

Proverbs 31:1-9 records some straight teaching that the mother of Lemuel, the king, gave him. His respect for her is immediately apparent in his reference to her words as an "oracle." Oracles were usually considered to be equal to prophetic utterances in the Old Testament. Most children today do not give parental instruction such respect.

We heard a preacher tell a story about a little boy who wandered away from home. His mother frantically searched for him but to no avail. She finally called the police, and headquarters notified a police helicopter that happened to be flying in that area at the time. The flying officer began a low circuit around the boy's neighborhood, and every few minutes he called out over a loudspeaker, "Johnnie Smith, go home." Soon Johnnie appeared on his own doorstep.

His mother discovered that he had been at a neighbor's, and she asked, "What made you come home?"

In great seriousness and awe he replied, "God told me to!"

Lemuel's mother addressed her son with great warmth and tenderness, "O my son, O son of my womb, O son of my

"You'll have to admit that our band director really knows how to get his students to do some focused listening."

vows [answer to my prayers]." Lemuel and his mother obviously had a close relationship. She took her role as a mother seriously. As the queen mother she didn't exploit her son's position and power for self-gratification or self-promotion. She had prayed for this son, and over the years she had earned the right to be heard. Lemuel's mother didn't say to him, "Now hear this and do as I say because I'm your mother." Instead, she built up credibility with her son over the years.

She communicated two basic life principles to her son: do not give in to excesses, and treat others fairly. Parents would do well to learn from her wise example of communicating with her son.

1. *Live your life with self-control.* She warned her son that although his position gave him power, it also carried a great weight of responsibility. "Do not spend your strength on women, your vigor on those who ruin kings," she said (Proverbs 31:3).

"It is not for kings, O Lemuel—not for kings to drink wine, not for rulers to crave beer, lest they drink and forget what the law decrees and deprive all the oppressed of their rights" (v. 4). A king was responsible for the welfare of his subjects. If he allowed his mind to be controlled by any substance, he would not be able to rule wisely. The people depended on the king to make good decisions, to execute justice.

This principle hasn't changed. Irresponsible living affects the lives of other people. The more people for whom a person is responsible, the greater the impact of his personal choices. Our minds are precious gifts from God. They are not to be wasted or destroyed. "Instead, be filled with the Spirit" (Ephesians 5:18).

Some years ago Winnie was invited to lead a Bible study for women in Alcoholics Anonymous. It was a great learning experience. One mother told Winnie that one of her teenage daughters had asked her to lie for her. The woman said, "My daughter had skipped school and gone to the beach with some of her friends. She asked me to write an excuse to her teacher saying she was sick that day. If she had come to me just a few weeks earlier with that request I probably would have done it.

I would have thought, *My life is so messed up, who am I to say to my daughter that it's wrong to tell a lie?* However," she went on, "I have hit a crisis in my own life. I'm dealing with my alcoholism. I am also working on my relationship with Jesus Christ. My life is turned around. So I said to my daughter, 'No, I can't lie for you. You'll have to take the consequences of skipping school.' Winnie," she concluded, "it felt so good to be right!"

That was precisely the point Lemuel's mother was trying to make. There is strength in moral integrity. A parent or leader's words will carry weight if they are backed by a disciplined life.

2. Lemuel's mother further charged, *"Commit yourself to justice and to defending the rights of the poor."* She taught her son to speak for those unable to speak for themselves. A leader sets the direction, and people listen. Lemuel's position as a leader was to serve the needs of the people. That is still what true leadership means: serving. "He who oppresses the poor shows contempt for their Maker, but whoever is kind to the needy honors God" (Proverbs 14:31).

Behind every person, no matter how lowly, is his or her Creator. Jesus reinforced that truth when He said, "I tell you the truth, whatever you did for one of the least of these brothers of mine, you *did for me"* (Matthew 25:40; italics added).

Lemuel's mother knew that the quality of her son's reign as king would not be determined by successful military conquests. Rather, it would be judged by his personal strength of character and his endeavors to help the weakest and poorest in his kingdom.

THINK IT THROUGH

What is your primary goal in your conversations with your children? Do you encourage them to develop into the best God has created them to be?

In what ways can you incorporate the concept of learning a new language into your home in the following areas: homework, manners, media habits, Bible reading, sports, music, and daily jobs?

SOMETHING TO DO

Think about political issues in your community. Do you voice opinions or sign petitions according to your self-interests or genuine commitment to the well-being of the poor in your community? What could you do about health, housing, education, illiteracy, elections, and poverty? What are you teaching your children about those issues?

11

Words and Family Conflicts

First go and be reconciled to your brother. (Matthew 5:24)

"Now what have I done?" "Can't I even speak?" "Get off my back will you?" "Stop hassling me!" Sound familiar? Words like those can be heard in homes across the country everyday.

We are all familiar with the fact of sibling rivalry. The term describes the pressure brothers and sisters exert against each other as they find their place in the world. In the animal realm it's called a "pecking order." Humans classify people according to "birth order" and try to give some rationale for varying attitudes and personalities.

A certain amount of verbal jostling between brothers and sisters is normal. The home is the natural setting for children to learn what it takes to get along in the world. When our kids were young, we heard a psychologist say, "If you don't allow your children to fight with each other when they are small, they will not be good friends when they are grown." Of course, the expert was not condoning violence or bloodshed—there are limits; but that was an encouragement to us at a time when we thought the bickering and arguments would never end.

It is instructive to see the reality of intense sibling rivalry recorded in Scripture. Jacob and Esau were twins with widely divergent interests and personalities. Jacob played the smooth operator, con artist, deceiver, and outright liar. He took advantage of his brother's weaknesses (cf. Genesis 25:27-34; 27). Esau's approach was more direct. "I will kill my brother Jacob," he said (27:41). Jacob fled the country but lived in fear for his life for many years (32:1-21; 33). He tried to appease his brother with gifts before they met again.

Jacob continued the cycle. He married two sisters and loved one more than the other. Both women vied for his attention and love. Leah, the rejected sister, longed for a closer relationship with Jacob that never seemed to materialize even though she bore him children. Rachel, the loved sister, had no children but played manipulative games to try to become pregnant (cf. Genesis 30:1-7). When Rachel's maid bore children to Jacob, Rachel's reaction was, "I have had a great struggle with my sister, and I have won" (v. 8). The struggle didn't end there, and the manipulation continued.

David was the youngest of eight brothers. That role in itself was full of pressure. The complaints at the beginning of this chapter came from the mouth of David and were addressed to his eldest brother, Eliab.

David's three oldest brothers had joined the army and were engaged in a war with the Philistines. David went back and forth between home and the battlefront taking food to his brothers and bringing back reports to his father. It was on one of his forays to the battlefield that David saw how the Philistine giant Goliath had totally demoralized and immobilized the armies of Israel. David was horrified because he viewed Goliath's challenge as a direct affront to the living God of Israel. As David tried to gather information, Eliab became furious and threw angry barbs at his youngest brother: "Why have you come down here? And with whom did you leave those few sheep in the desert? I know how conceited you are and how wicked your heart is; you came down only to watch the battle" (1 Samuel 17:28). Talk about slicing and cutting and spitting out words! If words could maim, those certainly could have rendered David helpless.

Eliab may have been jealous because he had been by-passed to be the next king (cf. 16:6-7). Instead, he'd witnessed David's anointing for that coveted honor. He was obviously under stress due to fear and the stalemate the Philistines had produced in the armies of Israel. He may have been trying to protect his youngest brother from getting hurt. Whatever his motive, Eliab attacked David's person, making serious charges against him. The Lord kept those words on record. Centuries later we are still reading them.

It was to that outburst that David responded with the words we have quoted—"Now what have I done? Can't I even speak?" In other words, "Get off my back, big brother!"

Older brothers and sisters tend to accuse the youngest of getting by with things they never got away with. They accuse the parents of showing favoritism to the baby and sometimes pick on the youngest to "get back." When they were young, our three older children ganged up on their youngest sister and verbally teased her unmercifully. They coined a derogatory name for her and refused to tell her what it meant. Thankfully, they outgrew their childish behavior.

Part of the human struggle springs from the inner longing we have to find favor with God, to please our parents, and to be recognized and accepted by our peers or siblings. If children can resolve those conflicts and relationships at home, they will become mature adults who are able to function in society.

However, if such conflicts are not resolved, the conflicts may be passed from one generation to the next. A number of years ago we visited some friends who were living in Europe. They had rented a house, and the wife had determined to make friends with their neighbors. However, the family next door refused to talk to her and turned their backs and walked away every time she approached. Our friend persisted and finally broke through that barrier of silence and hostility. She discovered that the owners of the home that they were renting had a long-standing feud with the family next door. In fact, the two families had not spoken to each other in one hundred years. Each generation had been indoctrinated regarding the quarrel, but it had gone on so long that the original reason for the feud had probably been forgotten.

Isaac and Rebekah established poor patterns of communication that kept surfacing in subsequent generations. They were perpetuated through their sons. It was years later before one of their grandsons, who had been most severely mistreated, finally began to resolve the sibling rivalry.

Jacob, Joseph's father, had put Joseph at an unfair advantage (or disadvantage) by showering him with attention to the exclusion of Joseph's older siblings. The writer of Genesis summed up the feelings of Joseph's brothers in this statement: "When his brothers saw that their father loved him more than any of them, they hated him and *could not speak a kind word to*

"THE FUNNY THING IS THAT THEIR FAMILIES HAVE BEEN FEUDING FOR SO LONG, NOBODY KNOWS WHAT THE ORIGINAL FIGHT WAS ABOUT."

him" (37:4; italics added). They wanted to kill Joseph but ended up selling him as a slave.

As a young man, Joseph chose to establish a personal relationship with God. That relationship carried him through the years of hatred in his home and the subsequent years of unfair treatment in Egypt.

After years of separation from his family, Joseph revealed what had been uppermost in his thinking during that time. He was not preoccupied with revenge and didn't say, "Just wait until I get my hands on my brothers." Instead, he said to his brothers, "Come close to me. . . . I am your brother Joseph, the one you sold into Egypt! And now, do not be distressed and do not be angry with yourselves for selling me here, because it was to save lives that God sent me ahead of you. . . . So then, it was not you who sent me here, but God" (Genesis 45:4-5, 8). The same thoughts are repeated in Genesis 50:19-21 with this additional comment: "And he reassured them and spoke kindly to them."

Joseph spoke kindly to his brothers who had not said a kind word to him. He exemplified what the New Testament means by the words "speaking the truth in love" (Ephesians 4:15). He didn't gloss over the evil his brothers had done. He acknowledged that what they had done was wrong but added, "You intended to harm me, but God intended it for good" (50:20).

Joseph didn't let his brothers make him bitter or angry. David didn't let Eliab's harsh words discourage him. Both men performed the jobs they knew had to be done. They did not attempt to prove a point to their families; instead, they wanted to honor God. Painful conflicts in their homes didn't destroy them. Because they each trusted God, the Lord built strength of character in both of them. If God can't overrule the evil that people do to one another, then He is limited in His power. Neither Joseph nor David believed in a limited God. They trusted an omnipotent, loving, and just God who can turn the anger of men to praise Him. Traumatic childhood or unfair treatment do not have to cripple anyone permanently. God is in the business of redeeming the worst of people and making them whole. He is also in the business of restoring broken relationships.

When brother and sisters make cutting remarks, there is no need to give up or get depressed. The way to keep normal sibling rivalry and jostling from deteriorating into injurious hostility is to establish a personal relationship with God. Get a right perspective through God's long-range view.

Both Joseph and David saw the larger picture, which helped them to rise above the immediate verbal barbs of their families. For "out of the overflow of the heart the mouth speaks" (Matthew 12:34).

THINK IT THROUGH

Think about your relationships with your brothers and sisters. Do you talk with each other? If not, why not? Be honest—are you jealous because they seem to have received more advantages than you? Are you envious of their gifts? Their beauty? If there is a breach is it because they actually abused you in some way, or were you guilty of such activity? Are you prepared to forgive them or to approach them to forgive you?

SOMETHING TO DO

Start the process of healing. Tell the Lord exactly what you understand the conflict to be. Ask Him to instruct you as to what to do. Write a letter to your brother or sister today asking him or her to help you work on reconciliation. Use the experiences of David and Joseph to help you. Hold on to that letter for a while, and allow the matter come into better focus. If there are no more changes to be made, send it with your prayers and in faith. Be prepared for God to act.

If the breach between you and your brothers and sisters has a long and ugly past, you may need to seek out a Christian counselor to guide you in the process of healing.

12

Crippling Words of Power in the Local Church

I fear that there may be quarreling, jealousy, outbursts of anger, factions, slander, gossip, arrogance and disorder. (2 Corinthians 12:20)

A schoolteacher joined a church with his family. He was a new believer, and he noticed that differences of opinion in the congregation were rarely verbalized out in the open. Instead, they were passed along in small groups, one-on-one, over the phone, or in prayer groups. They were disguised as "deep concerns" but often packed with innuendo and unverified statements. "As far as I am concerned that is merely power politics at work, plain and simple," he said.

It is an oxymoron to find warm fellowship and an underlying layer of rumor and doubt in the same church. Instead of using gracious and powerful words to encourage and strengthen the Lord's work, some Christians cripple the congregation. How does cruel innuendo find such easy lodging where, of all places, the opposite should be true?

"If you keep on biting and devouring each other, watch out or you will be destroyed by each other" (Galatians 5:15).

"*WHAT A SHOT! ONE ARROW LAUNCHED AT RANDOM AND HE TAKES OUT THE PASTOR, SUNDAY SCHOOL SUPERINTENDENT, JANITOR AND CHURCH SECRETARY!*"

Paul made that charge against *Christians*. The apostle repeatedly addressed this issue because he realized how divisive uncontrolled tongues could be. But the problem wasn't new to his day. Jealousy, rivalry, and power politics began much earlier in the congregation of God's people.

When the people of Israel were being organized into a nation, two dynamic leaders began to talk against Moses, God's appointed leader. They chose to gossip about his marriage, but that wasn't the primary issue. Rather, it was a power struggle. Miriam and Aaron resented the fact that Moses had risen above them to become the leader, and they asked, "Has the Lord spoken only through Moses? . . . Hasn't he also spoken through us?" (Numbers 12:2).

Because they wanted Moses' position they were willing to corrupt the thinking and attitudes of the rest of the people with their gossip. Because of personal jealousy they were willing to drag everyone else down to their level.

In that situation the Lord nipped the conflict in the bud. What Miriam and Aaron had said behind backs and closed doors, the Lord heard. At once He confronted them publicly. God challenged them, "Why then were you not afraid to speak against my servant Moses?" (v. 8). Moses was in that position because God had placed him there. The Lord also gave Miriam and Aaron high credit for their leadership alongside of Moses (Micah 6:4). Yet their jealousy got in the way.

We're told that the Lord's anger was hot against them, "and he left them." Miriam was struck with leprosy and became an outcast to the people she had served so well. That sounds like brutal treatment for such a minor offense; after all, she hadn't killed anyone or even stolen anything. But the incident gives us a vivid picture of how seriously God regards what we say and our motives for our words as well.

A list of things God detests includes these—pride, murder, lying, "and a man who stirs up dissension among brothers" (Proverbs 6:19). The Lord hates the division that gossip causes.

Aaron admitted his and Miriam's sin. He pleaded on Miriam's behalf. Then Moses prayed for his sister, and the Lord healed her after seven days. However, during those seven days, the whole congregation of Israel came to a halt.

We should be sobered by that account. Gossips lose their usefulness to the Lord. Divisive words hurt and corrupt other people. Hebrews 12:15 warns, "See to it . . . that no bitter root grows up to cause trouble and defile many." Gossip can hinder the progress of God's people, but restoration is possible if there is confession and forgiveness.

Paul heard some reports about the church in Corinth, but he didn't talk behind their backs. He addressed the people directly. Although Paul had received his position of authority from the Lord, he didn't try to build a power base for himself. He wasn't interested in creating a following. "For I am not seeking my own good but the good of many. . . . Follow my example, as I follow the example of Christ" (1 Corinthians 10:33–11:1).

Divisive words can be a way of exerting control, a form of power politics to gain a following or to maintain a position of influence in a congregation. Partisanship is not a new phenomenon in the church. The same problem caused jealousy, quarreling, and divisions in the church at Corinth. Paul wrote to the believers that such attitudes marked them as immature (3:1-4). He addressed this problem when he said to the Corinthians, "My brothers, some from Chloe's household have informed me that there are quarrels among you. What I mean is this: One of you says, 'I follow Paul'; another, 'I follow Apollos'; another, 'I follow Cephas'; still another, 'I follow Christ.'" Paul then asked this incisive question, "Is Christ divided?" (1:11-13*a*).

The three men Paul referred to—Apollos, Peter, and himself—were important leaders in the early church. By nature, people migrate to strong, dynamic leadership, and we see this in the church today. People follow the teaching of authoritative leaders and develop intense loyalty toward them. Unfortunately, this sometimes becomes a divisive force in the church body.

Christians need to be careful that they don't focus on their leaders and take their eyes off the Lord. As soon as we start following *people*, no matter how wise or spiritual they are, we open ourselves up to jealousy, rivalry, quarreling, divisions—the very things Paul warned against. That can happen on every level in a local church, from Sunday school teachers to elders and deacons.

Spiritually mature Christians recognize that even well-known Christian leaders and teachers are "only servants, through whom . . . the Lord has assigned to each his task" (1 Corinthians 3:5). Paul, Apollos, and Peter were merely doing what God had called them to do. Each focused primarily on Jesus Christ. None of them was any better than the others. God gave the assignment, God blessed their work, and God alone was to be magnified.

The fact that God had assigned each leader his responsibility did not negate the respect each leader deserved. In another letter Paul wrote specifically to that issue: "Now we ask you, brothers, to respect those who work hard among you, who are over you in the Lord and who admonish you. Hold them in the highest regard in love because of their work" (1 Thessalonians 5:12-13).

In his letter to Timothy, Paul added that showing respect for leadership included monetary support. "The elders who direct the affairs of the church well are worthy of double honor, especially those whose work is preaching and teaching. For the Scripture says, 'Do not muzzle the ox while it is treading out the grain,' and 'The worker deserves his wages'" (1 Timothy 5:17-18).

Leaders in the church need encouragement. They need support. When we sit in the back pews, we send a negative message to our pastors. How would you feel if people consistently chose to sit as far away from you as possible? It is a well-known fact that listening to a message is much more difficult from the back of the auditorium than from the front or midway through. From the rear there are too many distractions, such as children bobbing up and down or an old-timer dozing.

Another way to encourage leadership is to refer to specific points of the sermon. Too often Christians treat the pastor as an entertainer, saying, "That was a fantastic sermon, pastor!" When we are honest enough to admit, "That particular thought challenged me to do some serious thinking," or, "That point precisely applied to my situation," we are truthful, as well as supportive.

When your child tells you about something he has learned in Sunday school, be sure you tell the teacher. It's an encouragement to the teacher to hear that some of his lesson is getting through.

The congregation should not function as antagonists. The local church body is a living organism. Your hand or foot does not deliberately say to your arm, "I'm going to work against you today." Your foot is essential for the proper functioning of your whole person. The same is true in the church. We must avoid forming divisive parties. Remember, God assigns the tasks according to His desires, not because one person is more important than another. Unlike the world, God does not play politics, and members of the church need to keep that in mind.

Human beings are complex. Leaders and followers alike need to learn when and how to yield to one another, without sacrificing doctrine, so that they can function together as a healthy body. Local churches need spiritually healthy members who are active participants. Leaders need to acknowledge that followers need encouragement too. Each group needs the other.

First Corinthians 4 expands on this point. Paul was keenly aware that people who influence the lives of others can easily become proud. He reminded those who were tempted to honor one person over another, "Who makes you different from anyone else? What do you have that you did not receive? And if you did receive it, why do you boast as though you did not?" (v. 7).

Winnie recalls an incident that occurred when she was speaking at a meeting. She noticed a woman near the front of the audience scribbling furiously. Winnie thought, *She's really listening to what I'm saying and taking notes.* Afterward the woman approached her and asked, "Where did you get your dress? I sketched it hoping that I could find a pattern like it." Speakers can't afford to take themselves too seriously!

Pride is an insidious factor in power struggles. But sometimes it is a mask for insecurity. Gossip is an effective tool for an insecure person to maintain his or her position. The victims of such verbal tale-bearing can be scarred for life.

We interviewed a couple who had been victimized by pride and insecurity that led to gossip. Although the chain of circumstances occurred years ago, this couple is still enduring the consequences today. (We have changed some details to protect identities.)

Ed and Clare had left a large church to attend a smaller one in their community. They were impressed by the warmth and friendliness with which they were welcomed. In due time they became involved in Sunday school, worked with children's clubs, and Ed became a deacon.

It was as he assumed leadership that Ed became aware that the senior pastor seemed to be throwing up roadblocks. Instead of encouraging this young man to develop his gifts, he seemed to try to thwart them in one way òr another. Ed also noticed that the elders and other deacons rubber-stamped everything the pastor wanted. There was no discussion on any issue. Over a period of time, Ed noticed that several gifted men left the church, but he dismissed it as coincidence. As long as Ed steered clear of the pastor and avoided creating waves, things seemed to go well.

Unknown to Ed, however, as he became more and more involved in the church and people began to recognize him as a leader, the pastor was feeling more and more threatened. His resentment toward Ed grew.

One day Clare threw a surprise birthday party for Ed to which all their church friends were invited. People were slapping him on the back and hugging him with good wishes and congratulations. One of the guests who gave him a hug was the pastor's wife. The pastor saw this and apparently felt jealous. When the party was over, some of Ed's friends said to him, "What did you do? The pastor is fit to be tied!" Ed could not think of anything he had done that could have offended the pastor. The pastor never approached Ed on the issue, but he kept the pot simmering behind Ed's back.

One of Ed's gifts was working with boys, especially tough fellows from a rough neighborhood. Ed was a kind but firm disciplinarian. At one of the boy's club meetings, he grabbed a particularly disruptive boy by the shoulder. The boy retorted, "Get your hands off me, you fag!" Another boy heard the comment and repeated the comment to his mother. The mother phoned the pastor asking, "What kind of man is Ed?"

The fact that a question had been raised about his character got back to Ed. When he heard about it, he asked the pastor for the parent's name so he could speak with her directly.

The pastor refused to tell him. Instead, he let the false perception of Ed's being a homosexual grow. He even wrote to someone in another area and conveyed this innuendo.

When Ed heard from across the country the rumors circulating about him, he confronted the pastor, first on his own and then with two deacons present. The pastor then accused him of forcing his attentions on his wife and of being a homosexual. Neither accusation was true. Ed and Clare were sure that virtually no one else in the church would believe those reports either, including the pastor's wife, but no one was willing to stick his neck out to come to their defense.

Ed and Clare left that church. Their children, who were teenagers at the time, were embittered and angry over the way their father had been treated.

Now Ed and Clare say that instead of leaving, they should have forced the issue into the open by bringing up the situation before the congregation as the Scripture instructs in Matthew 18:15-17. They realize that it might have been better to expose the real problem for what is was—a power struggle. The pastor felt threatened by anyone who showed leadership potential, and he was willing to use innuendo and gossip to maintain control.

Ed was a deacon. Some serious charges were made behind his back. No witnesses were ever brought to him who could back those charges with evidence. Fooling around with the pastor's wife and being a practicing homosexual or pedophile are serious issues that should have been dealt with scripturally if they had been true.

On the other hand, Ed charged the pastor with making false accusations about him. That would be a serious charge to make against anyone. He had brought two witnesses. Ed and Clare followed the guidelines in Matthew 18:15-17 up to a point. According to Paul's recommendation they should have made it public, yet in mercy they chose not to. At the time they were more concerned about not creating division. Making any kind of charge against a church leader is serious business, not to be taken lightly as Paul's words confirm: "Do not entertain any accusation against an elder unless it is brought by two or three witnesses. Those who sin are to be rebuked publicly, so that the others may take warning" (1 Timothy 5:19-20).

Such situations, which evolve as a result of gossip, are extremely painful. The motives for correcting the situation have to be kept above board all the time, especially for the victim. The motivation behind making such a charge must not be merely to justify oneself, to set the record straight, or to get revenge. Rather, the victim should desire to see the perpetrator helped, restored, and built up, in addition to seeing him become all that God has redeemed him to be. The victim also needs to recognize that he may need to make some changes himself. Perhaps there are aspects of his personality or actions he committed that contributed to the other person's feelings of inadequacy.

Ed and Clare said that to this day the pastor has never admitted any wrongdoing. In fact, he gives a totally different account as to why they left the church. Yet they have forgiven him. They hold no bitterness or anger toward him. They pray for his health and spiritual well-being and that the church will prosper. They have gone on with their lives and are being used by the Lord in ways they wouldn't have anticipated before.

THINK IT THROUGH

What sphere of influence or opportunity has the Lord entrusted to you in your church (see Nehemiah 8:3)? In what ways can you avoid resenting someone else whose sphere may be larger than yours (see 1 Corinthians 12:14-26)?

How can you thwart the divisiveness that comes from gossip and power struggles in your local church (1 Thessalonians 5:14-22)? What scriptural principles relating to power struggles can you apply to your situation from Numbers 12 and from Paul's statements in 1 Corinthians 1:10?

SOMETHING TO DO

When did you last drop a note to your Sunday school teacher, growth group leader, or pastor to say thank you? Mail one this week. When did you last alter a conversation that began to destroy the work of God? Do so this week.

13

Overcoming Gossip and Inequities in the Church

Speak to one another with psalms, hymns and spiritual songs. Sing and make music in your heart to the Lord, always giving thanks to God the Father for everything. (Ephesians 5:19-20)

Speak, sing, make music, give thanks for everything. It sounds so wonderful. In such a spiritually uplifting atmosphere problems still develop because local churches are composed of people. Where there are people, there are usually problems and conflict. Wherever the Spirit of God is at work, so is the enemy trying to bring discord.

Prayer meetings can become fertile ground for gossip. We believe in prayer, in praying specifically, and in being honest. But we also believe in using caution and discretion. Prayer meetings can and should be constructive power houses. Unfortunately, they can also be forces for destruction. We have heard this comment more than once: "I don't go to that prayer group anymore because it's just a gossip session."

People are told to be specific in their prayers. Don't just generalize saying, "God bless our missionaries," or, "God bless John and Mary." Missionaries, for example, usually list specific requests in their letters, which are helpful. It *is* important to be specific. However, restraint is also needed.

We need to learn to avoid too much discussion about prayer requests before praying. In giving the request sometimes we tell more about the situation than anyone else needs to know. If someone in the group is sharing a personal need, the others in the group can be sympathetic listeners, but don't let that person give all the intimate details.

In our society it is popular to be open and honest and to "let it all hang out," but we reveal far more than we should. In *Woman's Day* Jo Coudert wrote an article titled "Secrets I'd Rather Not Know." She said that too often people reveal intimate details, such as a history of sexual abuse, the rape of a daughter, or time spent in a drug rehab center, on their first meeting. Ms. Coudert acknowledged that such candor is part of the new openness that is supposed to sweep away the repressions of the past. "Confession may be good for the soul," she said, "but it's not always good for the listener—or the relationship.[1]"

Small prayer groups often seem to be a safe haven for people to open up and express their needs. We have found, however, that later people regret saying so much. They may be embarrassed enough that they avoid those people in whom they confided. We need to protect one another from saying too much in the moment of crisis. In response to those who do share deep personal needs in a group, each member of that group should receive that information as a sacred trust. Don't pass it along to anyone else. Instead, keep lifting that request to the Lord in private prayer.

Praying for "John and Mary" raises another issue. Although people may know their marriage is in trouble, there is no reason for anyone to pray, "Lord, help John to stop fooling around," or, "Help Mary to stop drinking so much." Even saying, "Lord, you know the personal problems John and Mary are having," may betray a confidence. All kinds of ideas are transmitted through innuendo.

1. Jo Coudert, "Secrets I'd Rather Not Know," *Woman's Day,* August 15, 1989.

Prayer can also be a subtle form of criticism. Sometimes when an individual prays, "Please help our pastor in his visitation," his underlying meaning is, "He's not visiting the sick as he should be," or, "He hasn't come to see *us* in months." Another prays, "Give the pastor and deacons wisdom in making decisions," but actually means, "I don't approve of the changes they are making," or, "I wish they would move a little faster." Even asking God to "help us to have unity in our church" may be an underhanded way of saying, "These other people better come around to my way of thinking."

"A gossip betrays a confidence; but a trustworthy man [woman] keeps a secret" (Proverbs 11:13). A simple way to avoid gossip is to focus on keeping confidences. Both of us have been approached individually many times by people who want us to pray about certain situations. When such has been given to us in confidence, we don't even tell one another what has been said unless we get permission from the person who told us.

One pastor jokingly said from the pulpit, "If any of you have secrets, don't tell me. I'm likely to announce it on Sunday!" His glib attitude regarding something that serious in public indicated that that pastor was probably not trustworthy in private. We have had people tell us in great distress that things they confided to their pastor or Sunday school teacher have come back to them through a spouse or even the children of the one they originally confided in. That is betrayal, and it is wrong. The writer of Proverbs said, "A gossip betrays a confidence: so avoid a man who talks too much" (20:19).

That should never happen among God's people. "I know if I tell you this, it will never go beyond you" is one of the greatest compliments that can be paid a believer.

Even innocuous and "innocent" information is dangerous to pass along. For example, someone you know has gotten a promotion at work, bought a new car, is getting married, is pregnant, is moving. If it is a happy transitional occurrence, let the people involved have the joy of spreading the good news. We shouldn't deprive them of that pleasure. It is so easy to fall into the trap of wanting to show we are privy to information that we give in to the urge of passing it along.

That is true of bad news as well, perhaps even more so. We heard about a woman who had an accident in her home. Winnie saw that woman's son the same day and said, "We were so sorry to hear about what happened to your mother." He hadn't been home from work yet, and his wife hadn't been able to reach him to tell him what had happened. This thoughtless comment deprived the wife of sharing an important incident personally with her husband. You may think that's really stretching the point. No great harm was done. But we do believe that it emphasizes the importance of developing great sensitivity about what we are saying, to whom, and why, before we open our mouths.

Sometimes churches are guilty of unfair practices that need to be confronted. What can Christians do when situa-

"MARIE, DEACON SMITH IS AT IT AGAIN!...
...No, I WOULDN'T CALL HIM A GOSSIP—
HE'S MORE LIKE A TOXIC WASTE DUMP!"

tions develop that need some kind of corrective action? We have seen various responses. Some are stoic. Others are indifferent. They say, "There's nothing I can do about it anyway, so why get an ulcer over it?" Others get angry and hostile, even violent. Many do nothing more than complain, "It is so unfair!"

Often Christians just start griping. One woman told us that she could have been the original "dial-a-gripe." She could bend anyone's ear with a long litany of complaints about everyone and everything. That is not an effective tactic in the local church, although it is used often enough.

What scriptural guidelines can believers follow when confronted with inequities in the Body? The Bible gives an account of five women who were faced with an apparent injustice in the law. They lived at a time in Israel's history when the nation, having been delivered from slavery in Egypt, was on the brink of entering the land God had promised them. This new land was going to be divided up into tribal territories.

According to the law, ownership of land passed from father to son as a family inheritance. This law created a problem for the five women in this story. They were sisters whose father, Zelophehad, had died in the desert, and they had no brothers. Consequently, there was no one to claim the inheritance their father would have passed on. The law said that property could not be claimed by daughters. In the midst of the excitement and anticipation of entering a new land, the women realized there would be nothing in the future for them. In addition, their father's name and his place in the clan would disappear because he had no sons. It was a situation that was both unfair to their father and to them.

According to the account in Numbers 27, those women didn't go around verbalizing their feelings and complaints to other people. They didn't get angry, emotional, or violent. They didn't waste their energy wringing their hands and complaining. They were thoughtful women, and they knew the law. They knew the circumstances of their father's life and of his death in the desert. They understood God's dealings among the people. They were bold, but their boldness was based on knowledge. They knew what they were talking about. Then they went through the right channels to present their case. Based on thoughtful, calm logic they presented their concern to Moses. "Why should our father's name disappear from his clan because he had no son? Give us property among our father's relatives" (Numbers 27:4). Their words were logical, concise, and to the point. They didn't harangue or argue.

It must have taken tremendous courage (it probably helped that there were five of them) for those women to present their case publicly and in front of all the national leaders. Such a demand had never been made before. The inequity in the law had never been confronted. And Moses didn't know how to handle the case. So he took it to a higher court—God Himself.

The Lord's response was quick. He said, "Those women are right . . . change the law." From that time on if a man died in Israel leaving no sons, his property was to be given to his daughters.

Later, in Numbers 36, we see how reasonable the women were. When another issue was raised, they were willing to yield to protect tribal boundaries. "Zelophehad's daughters did as the Lord commanded Moses" (v. 10).

That episode in Israel's history represented a rule change that affected the whole congregation. They would have to change their thinking about certain aspects of their life.

The incident also illustrated Moses' wise leadership. He didn't jump to hasty conclusions or say, "That's the way it has always been. Sorry." He listened to the sisters with genuine respect and gave their case careful consideration. And when he wasn't sure what to do, he wasn't ashamed to admit he didn't know the answer and would have to get higher counsel. He was flexible enough to follow through and make changes.

THINK IT THROUGH

What principles can you apply from that story in dealing with gossip and conflict in your church? What steps can you take to correct a situation? What channels would be appropriate to use? As a church leader, how can you improve your handling of difficult situations in your congregation? What does Moses' example say to you personally?

SOMETHING TO DO

For two days jot down important topics you talk about in personal conversation, on the phone, or in a group—whether social, prayer, or Bible study. Ask yourself, *Why did I say that? Was it necessary? What did it accomplish? How can I improve my conversation next time?*

Next time you are in a prayer meeting, offer suggestions on how to pray specifically without revealing all the details. Urge your fellow pray-ers to maintain confidences. Resist the temptation to use knowledge of a personal nature as a subject of gossip.

14

Attacked by Criticism

Does not the ear test words as the tongue tastes food?
(Job 12:11)

How often do you express appreciation for your taste buds? Probably seldom. Taste is one of the five senses we take for granted. We appreciate food that tastes good and reject that which doesn't appeal to our palates. Taste buds do the work and send the appropriate signals to the brain. If we ate only foods with tastes we liked, we would probably suffer from malnutrition. Most children, if left to themselves, would happily try to exist on a diet of cookies, candy, potato chips, and soda. A healthy, balanced diet has to be taught. Acquiring a "taste" for nourishing food is a learned process.

Similarly, our sense of hearing must become equally discerning. Hearing and understanding what we hear is important. When Jesus told the parable about the sower, His emphasis was on the four different kinds of soil that received the seed. His application of the story concluded with these words, "Consider carefully what you hear. . . . With the measure you use, it will be measured to you—and even more" (Mark 4:24). We should become discerning listeners.

It is important to acquire the ability to hear what is said within the total context so that we can knowledgeably test the words. This duty becomes especially important when we hear criticisms directed at us. How can we apply this principle when we are the victims of harsh words?

After Job suffered his tragedies, he received a verbal barrage from his friends. They were attempting to find a reason for Job's suffering. Unfortunately, their answers were falling wide of the mark. They criticized Job's life and character because they could see no other rationale for what was happening to him. In their narrow scope of thinking this was their equation: suffering equals judgment from God. God judges sin; therefore Job must have sinned. In their minds the sooner Job recognized and acknowledged his sin, the faster God would lift His hand of judgment. Much of what they said would have been true in the appropriate situation. God is holy, and He does judge sin. Sinners suffer the consequences of their sin, and they need to repent. What his friends didn't realize was that Job's suffering was really the result of his *upright* life, not his waywardness.

People often judge and criticize others because their perspective is narrow. Several years ago we attended the graveside service for a niece who had died shortly after birth. The little casket was placed into the ground next to the graves of our first two children, who had each lived only three days. Our niece also had a brother buried in the plot next to hers. He, too, had lived only a few hours. The burial sites had been purchased by Chuck's father in preparation for his own death, but four of his grandchildren preceded him into those graves.

There were only a few family members and close friends at the funeral, and Winnie wept through the whole service. The memories of our own grief and pain were overwhelming. She felt sadness for the parents of this little one as well. After the service the officiating minister said to the baby's father, "I'm really worried about your sister-in-law, Winnie. I think she's losing her faith." He based that assumption on the fact that she had cried. The preconception on which he based his judgment was that strong Christians don't grieve, and if they do, they don't let it show.

Similarly, Eli, the Old Testament priest, made an assumption about Hannah and accused her of being drunk when she was actually crying to God in great anguish (see 1 Samuel 1:12-16).

Chuck has often used the phrase "selective perception" to describe the narrow scope through which people perceive what they wish to hear, read, or see. We listen to speakers, especially politicians or preachers, with our auditory antennae tuned in to certain ideas. We make quick judgments if they use certain terms in their rhetoric. The well-known cliché is true of too many people: "Don't bother me with the facts; my mind is already made up."

Destructive criticism, funneled through the critic's selective perception, can be motivated by any number of things: jealousy, dissatisfaction over circumstances, anger, unbelief, fatigue, feelings that God doesn't care, wrong priorities, or lack of knowledge about all the contributing factors in a situation.

We have already seen tunnel vision demonstrated in Miriam and Aaron's criticism of Moses. They talked against his wife behind his back, but God pinpointed the actual complaint: they envied Moses' position as leader. Perhaps their preconceptions were shaped by the long years Miriam and Aaron had suffered through slavery. They had come up through the ranks as slaves, so they had earned their right to be leaders among the people. They had proved themselves. In contrast, their younger brother, Moses, had lived a privileged life. His rash act of murdering an Egyptian at age forty had added another forty years to their bondage while Moses matured in relative peace in the desert. Yet God chose Moses, the youngest and apparently least experienced, to be top leader of the people.

Martha used a similar tack when she was upset with her sister, Mary. She didn't talk to Mary directly. Instead, she made her verbal outburst about Mary to Jesus, but she did it in Mary's hearing (Luke 10:38-42).

Through the years we have seen many people use these tactics to criticize others. We have been guilty ourselves. Criticism aimed at a particular person or group is done behind backs or through a third party. We know of two sisters who didn't like each other, and they communicated their criticism through a close relative who maintained contact with each of them. The relative was supposed to make each sister comply with the other's wishes. It didn't work.

Children are masters of this form of manipulation. A child complains to a mother about what his sibling is doing. The complainer wants the parent to punish or force the other child to comply with his wishes. We may say, "That's to be expected with children." But that behavior is carried into adulthood. For example, how many times have you complained to the pastor about someone else in the church instead of going directly to the person who is bothering you?

Indirect criticism can have devastating results. When Winnie began her nurse's training she had a roommate who was not a believer. In her desire to be a good witness Winnie was a little overzealous. She tried to be reasonable, but it turned out that her practice of reading her Bible and praying began to grate on her roommate's nerves. Instead of saying anything to Winnie about this, her roommate complained to a nursing supervisor that Winnie was trying to ram religion down her throat. Winnie happened to be working on that supervisor's floor at the time, and the first time she heard about her roommate's frustration was when the supervisor shouted at her, "You have no right to push your religion on anyone!" For the rest of her rotation that nurse made Winnie's life miserable. Her roommate left nursing school shortly thereafter. It became evident that it wasn't just Winnie's religion that was upsetting her when she returned to the hospital as a suicide attempt.

When we criticize another person, we are actually lodging a complaint against God Himself. He created that person in His image and therefore takes our words and actions seriously. We need to keep that perspective in mind. We have to be trained in a new mind-set.

God made this statement to Job's friends: "I am angry with you . . . because you have not spoken of me what is right, as my servant Job has." The men had to go to Job and rectify the situation with him before God. The Lord said, "My servant Job will pray for you, and I will accept his prayer and not deal with you according to your folly" (Job 42:7-8).

How did Moses deal with criticism? He had been a frequent target for complaints from the congregation he had led out of Egypt, as well as from his brother and sister. Yet in the situation with Miriam and Aaron, "Moses cried out to the Lord, 'O God, please heal her!'" (Numbers 12:13). A vengeful person would have said, "She's getting what she deserved," but Moses wasn't like that. He was able to see beyond the personal injury that the criticism caused him. *How will this affect her and everyone else?* he wondered. He thought through all the ramifications. He prayed for her restoration, and he repeatedly prayed for the complaining crowds (Numbers 11:1-2; 21:4-9).

How did Jesus deal with Martha's complaint? He didn't force Mary to comply with Martha's wishes. Instead, He forced Martha to confront her own attitude. Martha was so absorbed in her own needs and responsibilities that she couldn't see the larger perspective. Jesus didn't write Martha off or downgrade what she was doing. She was still a generous and hospitable woman. He merely challenged her to think through her priorities and to broaden her vision.

Where does constructive criticism fit into the picture? In the biblical accounts about Martha and Job's friends the Lord sets an example for constructive criticism. He addressed the persons and issues directly, not behind their backs or through a third party. His purpose was forgiveness and restoration, to build up and strengthen the spiritual perception of the criticizer, to make him or her useful again. God loves to restore strained relationships. Constructive criticism is not self-serving. It's motivated by love. It always wants to see the object of the criticism made better.

Before you verbalize your criticism to another person, ask these questions:

1. Why do I feel so upset about this person or issue?
2. Do I know all the facts?
3. Am I guilty of selective perception?
4. Am I going to gripe to someone else behind the person's back?
5. Am I trying to manipulate through a third party?
6. Do I love the person enough to have the courage to talk to him or her directly?
7. Is the criticism necessary, or am I just letting off steam?

How should you respond if you are the target of criticism? Think about the criticism. Is there any truth to it? What can you do to change?

Many years ago Winnie overheard someone asking a friend for some information about a family in the church. The friend responded, "Ask Winnie. If anyone knows, she does." It was not a compliment but an indictment. It was painful, and Winnie took it to heart. But she determined that from then on she was not going to be the source of information about people.

If the criticism isn't true, let it go by. Don't dwell on it. If you think about it too much, you will become bitter or angry. Moses got into trouble when he intercepted the people's criticism and took it personally. Actually their complaint was directed at God, not Moses. Moses should have ignored it.

Also, pray for the critic. Don't pray for God's judgment on him. Rather, pray for God's mercy and grace to be at work in the person's life.

Our Lord was the prime target of vicious and unjust criticism. "When they hurled their insults at him, he did not retaliate; when he suffered, he made no threats. Instead, he entrusted himself to him who judges justly" (1 Peter 2:23). We should do likewise.

THINK IT THROUGH

Reflect on Numbers 12 and Luke 10:38-42. Picture the settings, the words of criticism, and the outcomes. How can you apply the lessons from those situations to your own life?

SOMETHING TO DO

Write down a list of difficulties that exist in your family and in your world. Perhaps they are matters about which you have complained for some time. Now, across from that list write some possible solutions. Do some brainstorming. Look for the best solution to one problem. Commit that matter and action to God in prayer. Let the matter sit for a while, asking the Lord to work in the individuals' lives. Then with renewed confidence see if your solution to the problem works as you approach people to offer your help.

15

Honest Words in the Community

You are the salt of the earth. (Matthew 5:13)

A Sunday school teacher asked her pupils, "What is a lie?"

One little boy replied, "A lie is an abomination to the Lord, but it is a very present help in the time of trouble."

Children learn quickly how to lie. They become especially adept at lying when they see punishment looming. One of our young sons broke a window while playing ball. He was so convincing in telling the story he fabricated that we believed him. Then a neighbor who had seen the episode told Winnie what had really happened. At that point our son learned another biblical principle: "You may be sure that your sin will find you out" (Numbers 32:23).

Jesus identified Satan as the source of lies. "He was a murderer from the beginning, not holding to the truth, for there is no truth in him. When he lies, he speaks his native language, for he is a liar and the father of lies" (John 8:44). Satan's ultimate goal has always been to kill, destroy, and thwart God's purposes. He often uses carefully crafted words to achieve those ends. It was the power of his words, which sounded so reasonable, that deceived Eve in the Garden of Eden.

Lying is so common in our society that we don't seem to get upset about it. We assume that certain people are going to lie or exaggerate the truth, such as car salesmen, politicians, and advertisers. When they are caught in falsehoods we shrug our shoulders saying it merely proves our assumption. We tell "white lies" and think nothing of it.

One windy day in March we were drinking coffee at the kitchen table when we saw large pieces of our roof flying around our backyard! We discovered that the wind was tearing off portions of the roof, but the wind died down after a bit so major damaged was not sustained.

The insurance people came out to assess the damage. They suggested, "Why don't you make a claim for the whole roof?" Only about 10 percent of the roof had been torn away, but the thought was tempting. We knew we would eventually need a new roof, but it would not have been honest. So we said, "As Christians we can't make a claim for something that hasn't been damaged. We'll just ask for the lost section of the roof to be replaced."

Words do not have to be outright lies to fulfill Satan's purposes. They can be half-truths. Satan actively works to thwart the advance of God's redemptive program in the world. He uses people and their words.

In the Old Testament the enemies of God's people employed Satan's strategies to stop a building project: (1) They pretended to cooperate in the construction project so they could infiltrate the ranks and foil the project. (2) Then they tried to discourage the builders. (3) Next, they tried scare tactics. (4) They hired outside advisers to come and frustrate the builders. (5) They lodged a formal complaint to the king in Persia by writing a biased letter. (6) Finally, they used force to bring the work to a halt (cf. Ezra 4).

However, Satan doesn't have to utilize outsiders if he can find the right spokesperson within the ranks of believers. It is particularly sad when believers participate in telling lies, promoting falsehood, and deceiving others. We write an advice column in *Moody Monthly* magazine, and questions come to us from wives concerned about signing joint income tax returns with their husbands because they know their husbands are cheating on the forms. The husbands seem to get bolder each year because they have never been caught. The wives get more nervous because they are sure the Internal Revenue Service will catch up with them some time. Lying does not lead to peace of mind.

Such activity advances Satan's intentions. Christians who are consistently pessimistic, spread fear, doom, and gloom, or voice opposition at every initiative to advance the kingdom can bring God's work to a halt as effectively as any unbeliever.

When Jesus began to tell His disciples that His true mission on earth was to suffer, die, and rise again, Peter took Jesus aside and began to rebuke Him saying, "Never, Lord! . . . This shall never happen to you!" (Matthew 16:22). Peter verbalized, perhaps unwittingly, the intent of Satan to thwart in any way possible God's plan of redemption. It must have come as a terrible shock to Peter when Jesus replied, "Get behind me, Satan! You are a stumbling block to me; you do not have in mind the things of God, but the things of men" (v. 23).

Christians do not deliberately choose to be a mouthpiece for the devil. Yet we need to be aware of his devices so that we don't play into his hands. Lying, deceitful, unforgiving tongues give the enemy a foothold to bring ultimate death and destruction.

One of the most tragic stories in the Bible is recorded in 1 Samuel 21:1-9; 22:6-23. At that time David was running from Saul. One of Saul's men, Doeg, took a report to Saul that resulted in the massacre of eighty priests. David reflects on that incident in Psalm 52 and discusses Doeg's words, which had caused such carnage.

> Why do you boast of evil, you mighty man?
> Why do you boast all day long,
> you who are a disgrace in the eyes of God?

Your tongue plots destruction:
    it is like a sharpened razor,
    you who practice deceit.
You love evil rather than good,
    falsehood rather than speaking the truth.
You love every harmful word,
    O you deceitful tongue!
Surely God will bring you down to everlasting ruin.

Later in the psalm, David describes Doeg as "the man who did not make God his stronghold but trusted in his great wealth and grew strong by destroying others."

Doeg's words revealed his character. His character was developed in a life he chose to live apart from God; he focused on getting to the top, regardless of how many people he destroyed in the process.

In the early church one particular couple wanted people to believe that they were more generous than they really were. They lied about the profits from a sale of property. They pretended they were giving all the profits to the Christians. Peter challenged the husband, Ananias: "How is it that Satan has so filled your heart that you have lied to the Holy Spirit? . . . What made you think of doing such a thing? You have not lied to men but to God" (Acts 5:3-4). Ananias's wife concurred with the plan to lie, and they each died instantly, one after the other. Judgment seldom comes that quickly. Because judgment is delayed people can be lulled into a false sense of security, thinking that it will never come.

God is truth. Anything less than truth is not from God. When Jesus described the origin of lies, He was addressing people and leaders who took pride in their religious heritage. He told them, "You belong to your father, the devil, and you want to carry out your father's desires" (John 8:44). That was a strong indictment of those leaders who prided themselves on their piety. Jesus told the truth, and when confronted with truth that pious crowd tried to kill Him.

If Christians are to be salt and light in a world influenced by Satan's deceit, they must be committed to honesty on every level. "Truthful lips endure forever, but a lying tongue lasts only a moment" (Proverbs 12:19).

God will take into account not only what we say but also our motive for speaking. If the motive was to give a wrong impression or to deceive, then even if the statement is true, God will judge the motive and the intent. Doeg's motive was to deceive, kill, and destroy—all to promote himself. David said that God's judgment on such harmful words would be severe.

One of the Ten Commandments clearly states, "You shall not give false testimony against your neighbor" (Exodus 20:16). Lying affects society and the communities in which we live. True justice cannot be enacted in the midst of falsehood.

Proverbs 6:16-19 says that the Lord hates "a false witness who pours out lies." Biblical history records an example of false testimony that was used to deceive. Jezebel, the wife of Ahab, a king of Israel, used false witnesses to get rid of a landowner. As a result of that false testimony, the landowner was executed, and King Ahab acquired the man's property (1 Kings 21:1-14).

Christians have been victims of false accusations through the centuries by those who oppose Jesus Christ. Jesus warned His followers that this would happen, so we shouldn't be surprised by it.

False witnesses were used against Jesus in His trial. False witnesses brought charges against Stephen. In both situations, the person on trial lost his life. Death and destruction are always Satan's goal. With Jesus' death he probably felt he had finally triumphed. But Jesus rose again. Through His death and resurrection Jesus guaranteed that true justice and truth will ultimately prevail. We know that truth will ultimately triumph. But people's lives can be destroyed along the way.

We were told about a pastor and his wife who took pregnant teenagers into their home as a ministry for the Lord. One of the young women became angry at the couple about something and began spreading stories that the pastor had tried to rape her. She later confessed that she had made up the story, but in the meantime, the pastor had lost his church, his ordination, his ministry, and his reputation.

"Do not lie to each other, since you have taken off your old self with its practices and have put on the new self, which is being renewed in knowledge in the image of its Creator" (Colossians 3:9-10).

Learning a new language is learning to tell the truth. Honesty starts in small ways. Return the extra change that the cashier at the supermarket gives you by mistake. Encourage honesty in your children. We saw a negative example of this point in a restaurant. A man got up from his table to pay for his bill and dropped a $10 bill from his wallet without noticing. A little girl at the next table saw the money on the floor, quickly picked it up, and started after the man to return it. The mother grabbed the child and said in a hoarse whisper, "Come back here! He doesn't know he lost it. You found it. You keep it." The man apparently didn't miss the money as he paid his bill and left. But we felt very sad for that little girl. That mother's words and action crushed something valuable in her daughter's character. It's those small decisions that reveal, as well as develop, character.

People of integrity who speak the truth seem to be a disappearing breed. Followers of Jesus Christ, of all people, should be committed to truth. Since Chuck teaches at Moody Bible Institute, we always enjoy hearing reports from businesses in the city who employ Moody students. Statements such as this frequently come back to us: "We like to employ Moody students. They are the only people we can trust with our cash registers." Integrity can impact the community.

We have a friend who is a concrete finisher. For years he has quietly gone about his work. He is reliable and always does an excellent job. He is gentle, friendly, cheerful, kind, and does not tell dirty jokes or use off-color language. On one occasion a union representative asked to see our friend's union card because he couldn't believe a man like that was actually a union member. Our friend was being salt and light in a setting where his distinctive language made an impact.

Do your neighbors know they can trust you? Can they trust your word? Can they be sure you won't get angry or get even if their dog tramples your flowers or their child breaks your window? Does your speech reflect who you belong to? We heard a secular talk show in which several people made a plea for more old-fashioned courtesy and consideration in this generally rude and angry world. Those positive qualities of speech should come naturally to Christians.

In the midst of a crisis Paul spoke with quiet confidence to frightened shipmates: "The God whose I am and whom I serve stood beside me and said, 'Do not be afraid'" (Acts 27:23-24). Troubled neighbors will turn to people like that when crises come. For example, we had neighbors with whom we were friendly, but we had not developed a significant relationship. Then one day their baby died in a crib death. They came to us to find some consolation.

The people who annoy us and get under our skin are often hurting people. We need to be careful that we don't close the door against reaching them by being careless in the things we say to and about them.

Satan is a liar and destroyer, but the Lord gives life and hope.

> Lord, who may dwell in your sanctuary?
> Who may live on your holy hill?
> He whose walk is blameless,
>   and who does what is righteous,
> who speaks the truth from his heart
>   and has no slander on his tongue,
> who does his neighbor no wrong
>   and casts no slur on his fellow man.
>   (Psalm 15:1-3)

Satan is a killer, liar, deceiver, and adversary. No one has to be a mouthpiece for him willingly or unwittingly. Through His death and resurrection Jesus Christ triumphed over Satan, so we know that "the one who is in you is greater than the one who is in the world" (1 John 4:4).

THINK IT THROUGH

Read Psalm 52, which David wrote about Doeg. Write down all the descriptions he used about Doeg's tongue. How would God treat such evil speaking? How would believers respond? What do verses 8-9 reveal about David's relationship with God? How can those verses encourage believers who may have succumbed to lying and deceiving and even advancing Satan's cause by thwarting God's program? Where is our hope? Study 1 John 4:4-6.

SOMETHING TO DO

If someone has hurt you, perhaps by undercutting you in your job, determine kind words or a gesture you can extend to that person. Then, *do* it.

Read Romans 12:14-21. List some practical ways in which you can obey these instructions with your neighbors and colleagues this week. Then follow through on those ideas.

16

Growing in the New Language

You may participate in the divine nature. (2 Peter 1:4)

"What do you think is the most beautiful word in the English language?"

How would you answer that question? Take a minute and write down the words that come to mind.

The moderator of a radio program posed that question to a group of children. The youngsters were among the best and brightest selected to appear on a program called "The Quiz Kids." Week after week children were quizzed on a wide selection of topics, and their intelligent replies were amazing. On that occasion, as we recall it, there was a thoughtful silence for a few moments. Then a boy responded, "I think the most beautiful word in the English language is *forgiven.*" Thinking about it now after many years still evokes emotion.

We have discussed some painful, harsh, and challenging topics revolving around the power of words. As we examine the Scriptures we have realized how far short we fall in achieving God's high standards. Perhaps you feel the same way.

God tells the truth in the Bible. He tells the truth about Himself, about people, about what He hates, about what He wants. He doesn't do it to make us go into a tailspin of despair. Rather, He wants us to see the clear picture of who we are so that He can turn us around to radically change us into what we can become in Him.

The apostle Paul said, "Everything that was written in the past was written to teach us, so that through endurance and the encouragement of the Scriptures we might have hope" (Romans 15:4). Forgiveness, new life, new language, and building life-giving, hopeful words—all are possible to the person who is willing to let Christ transform him or her.

Peter wrote powerfully on this subject. The gospels reveal him as a man with many rough edges. Yet in spite of all the mistakes he made in what he said and did, a consistent characteristic ran through his life. He genuinely loved Jesus Christ and wanted to please Him. His example gives hope to all of us. The angry, deceitful, harsh, abusive, gossiping words we have spoken cannot be recalled. But they can be *forgiven*. And a new language—God's language—can be learned. Let us look at the characteristics Peter wrote about in his second letter specifically in the light of learning a new language.

Peter wrote his letter to believers, those who had already established a personal relationship with God through faith in Christ (2 Peter 1:1). That was the starting place. We all have to begin there. Romans 10:9-10 refers to a verbal expression of faith based on a heart commitment.

Once that relationship is established through faith Peter challenged his readers "to add to your faith." The thought is to add *lavishly* to your faith. Don't be stingy in expending your energy. Christ hasn't redeemed us to rest on our faith and coast into heaven. We are born again to grow, mature, and learn a new language.

When San Francisco was hit with the earthquake of October 17, 1989, television cameras focused on the most devastated areas. One police officer shouted instructions to people milling about in apparent confusion. He said, "Get prepared! There will be no utilities for seventy-two hours. Fill your bathtubs with water. You have ninety minutes of daylight left.

So get busy, and do what you have to do. Don't just stand here doing nothing!"

That, in effect, is what Peter communicated: "Don't just stand there doing nothing. You have faith. Now build on it." Then he reminded his readers what their resources were: "His divine power has given us everything we need for life and godliness through our knowledge of him who called us by his own glory and goodness. Through these he has given us his very great and precious promises" (vv. 3-4).

What are those resources? His "divine power" is the indwelling Holy Spirit. His "very great and precious promises" are the Scriptures. With those resources we have everything we need to learn a new language.

The purpose is "so that . . . you may participate in the divine nature and escape the corruption in the world caused by evil desires" (v. 4). We were created in the image of God, and now God is recreating us in the image of Jesus Christ. "For from the very beginning God decided that those who came to him . . . should become like his Son" (Romans 8:29; TLB). In addition, we are to avoid the destructive words prompted by greed and pride and self-interest.

Peter continues, "If you do these things, you will never fall, and you will receive a rich welcome into the eternal kingdom of our Lord and Savior Jesus Christ" (vv. 10b-11). He promises security for the present and hope for the future. God's goal is to build into us the character of Jesus Christ and to make us fit citizens of His kingdom. He wants us to be comfortable in that future environment in heaven.

We don't know whether we have ninety minutes or ninety years left to begin growing. The point is that we need to start now. For the Christian, conversion is just the beginning of a lifetime of growth. In the following diagrams the circle represents the circumference of life, with the center representing new life in God through faith in Christ. Growth from the center of life occurs through the resources of the Holy Spirit and the Bible.

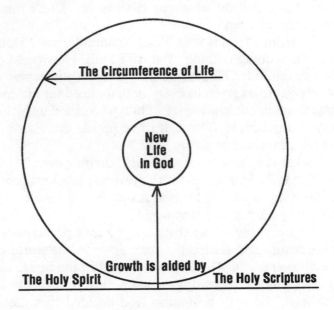

A growing relationship is nourished by the resources of the Holy Spirit and the Word of God. Drawing on those resources, Peter lists seven areas in this passage in which believers should be growing. They are not like rungs of a ladder that we climb one at a time. Rather, they are all character qualities that should be developing simultaneously.

> Make every effort to add to your faith goodness; and to goodness, knowledge, and to knowledge, self-control; and to self-control, perseverance, and to perseverance, godliness, and to godliness, brotherly kindness; and to brotherly kindness, love.

As we discuss these qualities, we will apply them primarily to language.

1. *Goodness*, or *virtue*. That word is also translated as moral excellence, or power. It speaks of strength of character. In the Old Testament the same concept is used to describe the well-known woman of Proverbs 31:10. It's the Hebrew word *chayil*, which means valiant, powerful, brave, and strong. It is used frequently in the Old Testament to describe "mighty men of valor [*chayil*]" and in such statements as, "through God we shall do valiantly [*chayil*]" (Psalm 60:12; NASB*).

It takes strength of character and courage to live by a standard different than the world around us. Romans 12:2 puts it this way, "Do not conform any longer to the pattern of this world." This is especially true when it comes to speech.

It not only takes courage to refuse to be drawn in by the world, but it takes great strength to speak up for what is right and true especially if your life is in danger. On one occasion, Peter and John were seized by the authorities when they were preaching. They were challenged, "By what power or what name did you do this?" Peter made his reply "filled with the Holy Spirit" (Acts 4:8). Peter was calm. He didn't panic, as he had done before. He was drawing on the resource of the indwelling Holy Spirit. Peter finished speaking, and "when

---

* *New American Standard Bible.*

[the religious authorities] saw the courage of Peter and John and realized that they were unschooled, ordinary men, they were astonished and they took note that these men had been with Jesus" (Acts 4:13). They were speaking a new language with the power that was the outflow of lives of moral integrity, goodness, and virtue.

Many stories have been told through the centuries of men and women who have taken courageous stands for the gospel and suffered severe consequences. It's not comfortable to think about such possible results. Nevertheless, moral excellence, strength of character, and goodness are to be added lavishly to our faith. Positive, verbal expression requires courage.

A beautician became a Christian through a Bible study group. She soon discovered through the Scriptures that "rendering to Caesar what is Caesar's" meant paying income taxes honestly. Everyone else in the shop declared the minimum amount they owed for the tips they received, but the new Christian decided to keep track of her tips. She discovered she was making far more than what she had been claiming. So she declared the true amount, which meant that she had to pay more taxes. Her boss told her she was a fool. The other employees got angry because they feared that their dishonesty would be discovered. Life was made miserable for a time for the Christian. She went quietly about her work, and she prayed for the other employees. Gradually the others began to trust Christ because of her gentle, strong witness. She drew upon the resources that God had given to her. She didn't harangue or preach at the others. She merely did what was right, and God did the rest. When the others came into new life in Christ, they too began to pay their taxes honestly. Government and society benefit from Christians who live out their Christianity.

2. Knowledge. Know what you are talking about before you speak. Peter understood that well. When Jesus was transfigured and Moses and Elijah appeared on the mountain with him, Peter had said, "Let us put up three shelters—one for you, one for Moses and one for Elijah. (He did not know what he was saying)" (Luke 9:33). All three disciples on that mountain were frightened, but it was Peter whose mouth ran ahead of his brain. "It is not good to have zeal without knowledge, nor to be hasty and miss the way" (Proverbs 19:2).

Earlier we discussed Zelophehad's daughters, who built their case on knowledge. They knew the law. Our knowledge is built on the Scriptures. If you have never made a plan for consistent reading and study of the Word of God, we encourage you to do so. It is absolutely impossible to learn God's language with a closed Bible. Make a plan for personal reading that will cover the Bible from Genesis to Revelation. Don't skip anything. "All Scripture is inspired by God and profitable for teaching, for reproof, for correction, for training in righteousness" (2 Timothy 3:16; NASB).

Parents, teach your children the Scriptures. The more you absorb God's Word and talk about it in your home, the more it will affect the way you speak to one another. We should remember Jesus' admonition to leaders of His day, "Are you not in error because you do not know the Scriptures or the power of God?" (Mark 12:24).

3. *Self-control.* Controlling the way we talk is not the norm in our society. People speak their minds and express their feelings. Self-indulgence on many levels is promoted, advertised, and verbalized. There are few restraints.

Lemuel's mother gave sound advice. We should listen to her. Joseph restrained himself in talking to his brothers. If he had lashed out at his brothers in anger we would have said, "He had every right to do so for the way they treated him." Joseph had established a standard of self-control as a way of life. He expressed it in a question to his employer's wife, who kept trying to seduce him, "How . . . could I do such a wicked thing and sin against God?" (Genesis 39:9*b*). His self-control in his speech and his decisions emanated from his relationship with God. The more we yield to the Holy Spirit the greater will be our self-control. The Holy Spirit does not put people out of control. We lose self-control when we don't rely on the resources that God has given us.

4. *Steadfastness,* or *perseverance.* That is the charge to keep going when you feel like quitting. Jonathan remained true to David throughout their friendship. He kept on encouraging him although his own life was endangered by their relationship. Most of the time, though, it isn't the crises that get to us as much as the daily grind. Someone has said that "the primary problem with daily life is that it is so daily."

Perseverance is a word we don't hear about much in our culture. It is hard to keep on encouraging someone if we are weary ourselves or if the person we are trying to help refuses to be encouraged. It gets tedious. People do not usually choose endurance as a way of life. Friendships don't last. Marriages don't endure. Young people quit school. People change jobs. Church members leave churches.

In a previous chapter Winnie told of her experience during her first months of nurse's training when she almost decided to quit. But a challenge came to her from an unexpected source that cause her to think twice about her decision. Another student nurse had a father who was overtly agnostic. When he heard about Winnie's dilemma with her roommate and the pressure from the nursing supervisor he said, "Well, now is the chance for Winnie to show whether her faith is real or not." She accepted the challenge and stayed in school.

Winnie had many rotations on that nursing supervisor's floor, and on each rotation the relationship grew more cordial. Three years after graduation Winnie checked into that hospital to have our second child. Our first baby had died after three days, and our second baby only lived three short days as well. That nursing supervisor was still working at the hospital, and someone heard her saying to some visitors, "You don't have to worry about Winnie. Her faith will hold her."

Perseverance has its rewards. Winnie's friend whose father was an agnostic also received the reward of perseverance. When her father was ninety and bedridden, his daughter cared for him. She patiently and consistently loved him, and he finally yielded his heart to Jesus Christ.

Perseverance in prayer reaps benefits, too. We received a letter from a pastor in China who said he had prayed faithfully for members of our family for more than fifty years. James wrote that those who persevered would "receive the crown of life that God has promised to those who love him" (1:12). Jesus endured the cross for "the joy set before him" (Hebrews 12:2).

5. *Godliness.* As children of God we should bear a strong resemblance to our heavenly Father. We heard a delightful story about a Sunday school student in the Philippines. The teacher had no pictures of Jesus to show the children and asked the children one Sunday, "What do you think Jesus looks like?" A little girl raised her hand and said, "I think Jesus must look like Mr. Brooks." Mr. Brooks was a missionary who was working in that area.

The authorities could tell that Peter and John had been with Jesus by the way they spoke and acted. "Train yourself to be godly . . . godliness has value for all things, holding promise for both the present life and the life to come" (1 Timothy 4:7-8).

6. *Brotherly kindness.* In God's family there should be genuine affection for other members of the family. Kindness cuts across the destructive forces of anger, rivalry, bitterness, power struggles, deceit, and gossip, which are so divisive in the Body of Christ.

When His disciples argued about who would have first place in the kingdom, Jesus told them to serve one another. They weren't to lord their position over each other. The world acts that way; the followers of Jesus don't.

Is there anyone in God's family with whom you aren't speaking? What can you do to bring about a reconciliation? Don't wait for the other person to make the first move. You do it.

In a small Bible study one morning, two of the women got into a heated discussion. Some sharp words were exchanged. After the study, one of the women involved was at home having her quiet time. She came to the verse in James that says, "Confess your faults to one another." She remembered the incident of the morning and considered phoning to apologize to the other woman. But she said to herself, *That woman was wrong, too.* She argued with herself and with the Lord for a while but finally gave up the struggle and picked up the phone. She asked the other woman to forgive her for what she had said. When she told us the story later, she said, "The hardest part was that the other woman accepted my apology without making one of her own."

Is there someone of whom you need to ask forgiveness? Do it. Verbalize it. The prodigal planned what he would say to his father. We should be just as specific when we ask the Lord to forgive us. "Take words with you and return to the Lord" (Hosea 14:2).

Is there someone you need to forgive? As long as you hold a grudge against another person you are allowing that person to maintain control over you. If someone has slighted, hurt, or ignored you, don't let your resentment build. Forgive. There is great freedom in going to church and not having to avoid anyone because of a breach in relationship. Refusing to forgive is a heavy burden to carry.

Do you need to forgive yourself? If Christ has forgiven you, the sin and the guilt is gone. Don't keep picking up the guilt again.

Look for ways in which you can express genuine appreciation for your brothers and sisters in Christ. How about the person who sets up the Sunday school chairs? Who makes sure there are supplies in the church kitchen? Who shovels the walks by the church when it snows? Look for people who do those things we take for granted. Say to them, "I really appreciate your faithfulness in . . . " A major aspect of the new language is learning to say thank you to one another. Verbally express genuine appreciation to the person who has a gift or responsibility you notice. Jesus said, "By this all men will know that you are my disciples, if you love one another" (John 13:35).

7. *Love.* The word Peter used here was *agape*, that highest form of unselfish, giving, "in spite of" kind of love. This was God's love.

Peter had come a long way in his journey of learning a new language. Peter's boasts that he would never leave Jesus or deny Him and that he would stay with Jesus to the end were sincere. He stated his intentions; he just didn't live up to them. His own failure was a crushing blow to him.

When Jesus met His disciples on the shores of the lake after His resurrection, He had a touching verbal encounter with Peter. He asked him, "Do you truly love [*agape*] me?" Peter's response: "Yes, Lord . . . you know that I love [*phileo*] you" (John 21:15). Peter used a more restrictive word, which essentially meant, "I have great affection for you."

We have heard many sermons on this passage in which the preacher paints Peter with a negative slant because he didn't use *agape* in his response. But perhaps Peter's great boasts and tragic denials were still so fresh in his mind that he thought, *I'm not going to claim I have that superlative love and risk not measuring up to that*. Whatever the significance, Jesus repeated Peter's word in verse 17 and went right on to tell him, "Feed my sheep."

Peter was not disqualified by his past verbal blunders. He was used as a dynamic preacher and leader in the early church. When he wrote his second epistle, he told his readers to add *agape* love lavishly to their faith. Peter had learned that if he could love with that superlative love so could his readers.

Peter continued, "For if you possess these qualities in increasing measure, they will keep you from being ineffective and unproductive in your knowledge of our Lord Jesus Christ. But if anyone does not have them, he is nearsighted and blind, and has forgotten that he has been cleansed from his past sins" (vv. 8-9).

Thus the chart enlarges on the results of spiritual growth in the circumference of life.

God is in the business of redeeming and restoring people. Indeed, the most beautiful word in any language is *forgiven*.

Words have power. Words endure. They give life and bring death. They reveal individuals. God can change every person and give him or her the resources to learn a new language that will glorify Him and strengthen His people.

"May the words of my mouth and the meditation of my heart be pleasing in your sight, O Lord, my Rock and my Redeemer" (Psalm 19:14).

Add lavishly to your faith in these areas. The new language can become as natural to you as your native tongue. Winnie's father grew up in the United States in a Swedish settlement. His native tongues were English and Swedish. Yet, in the final weeks of his life he spoke Chinese almost exclusively. He had spent more than fifty years in China and Taiwan as a missionary and became so adept in that language that he actually thought in Chinese. When he lost his hearing, he spoke English with Chinese intonations. He was as comfortable in that learned language as he was in his native tongues. We have all the resources we need to speak God's language as comfortably as Winnie's father did Chinese.

THINK IT THROUGH

Read 2 Timothy 3:1-5. List the attitudes in speech patterns described by Paul. Contrast this list with Peter's list in 2 Peter 1:5-9. In what practical ways do they differ? Give examples from your own life and experience.

Read 2 Timothy 2:24-26 and 3:10-17. What characterizes the speech of a Christian? Under what circumstances? To what resources does Paul refer?

SOMETHING TO DO

Make a plan for personal study of the Scriptures starting today. Our little book *How to Listen When God Speaks* (Shaw Publishers, Wheaton, Illinois) could give some guidelines. Put Colossians 3:16-17 into practice. Evaluate everything you hear by the principles you have observed in these studies. Then encourage fellow believers by passing along what you have learned.